COMPOST HAPPENS

Confessions of a Plantaholic

by
Shelly Hargis Murphy

Vabella Publishing
P.O. Box 1052
Carrollton, Georgia 30112

©Copyright 2012 by Shelly H. Murphy

All rights reserved. No part of the book may be reproduced or utilized in any form or by any means without permission in writing from the author. All requests should be addressed to the publisher.

Garden photos by the author unless otherwise noted.
Author's photo by McLain Photography.
Cover design by DianaBlack.com

Manufactured in the United States of America

13-digit ISBN 978-1-938230-03-5

Library of Congress Control Number 2012937088

10 9 8 7 6 5 4 3 2 1

For Ed, who supported me in so many ways

ACKNOWLEDGEMENTS

Just as numerous components are required for a seed to become a plant that bears flowers, so it is with a budding writer like me with a passion for growing ornamentals. Without proper nourishment from so many sources, this book could not have happened.

Initial gratitude is extended to those who taught my 2002 Master Gardener Class, everything from the fact fire ants eat termites to how compost happens, and the best advice of all—how to look up the answer.

I am grateful for knowledge gleaned from terrific programs, field trips and conferences as well as personal advice from friends in both state and local Master Gardeners and my Little Tallapoosa Botanical Society.

Thanks to Carrollton Creative Writers Club for programs and member input that are so helpful. I laud your critiques and relish your laughter. Much oblige to our mentor, Mary Saxon Wilburn, for forming this support group for writers, and to T.L. Gray for feedback and editing.

Special appreciation is owed to Eleanor Hoomes, Claire Baker, Donna Spivey and Joy Padgett, who meet with me monthly to expand our waistlines and writing egos, for providing positive reinforcement, as well as invaluable advice, critiques and editing.

Kudos to Ed and Bryan for eagerly eating speedy cuisine when dinnertime found me outside stuck in muck up to my eyeballs or still in my pajamas lost in thought at my computer. I am indebted to you both for your love, encouragement and support in this endeavor.

CONTENTS

PROLOGUE

It never occurred to me 20 years ago that I would ever be an avid gardener or an author. With a background in accounting and English, I'd opted to be a stay-at-home senior soccer mom to a newborn son whose two siblings were already in college, hoping to have more time for traveling and creative pursuits.

Though somewhat agri-curious as a child, I got a late start at serious gardening. In sharp contrast to most of my Master Gardener friends, who began gardening right out of the cradle with relatives, I was not so fortunate. I learned nothing about horticulture from my parents, who seemed to have an aversion to it from hardships associated with growing up on small Texas farms during the Great Depression and 1930's Dust Bowl. Their distaste grew even more acute after they moved to Carlsbad, New Mexico, when I was a toddler.

Those who have been there need no explanation. Though the state license plates proudly proclaim it "The Land of Enchantment," tourists often marvel how one can drive over 100 miles and never see a tree growing in the wild. My dad always claimed everything of worth in southeastern New Mexico was under ground—oil, potash, water and even the Carlsbad Caverns National Park, for which my home town is famous. Though the desert has a special kind of beauty—interesting rock formations, vivid sunsets, and beautiful mountains in the distance—green is not a prominent color in the natural landscape. With an average annual rainfall of 14 inches, it's obvious why gardening there is a challenge.

My father did make one attempt to grow vegetables at our first new home, primarily to save money. Though I was only four, I mainly remember his complaints about the poor rocky sandy soil, the high cost of water, the hard work and the pitiful results. The following spring, when he was 43, he had a heart attack. Though he lived to be almost 81, except for some pecan and apricot trees he planted in back when I was a teenager, Daddy never attempted growing food again. Though he admitted homegrown produce tasted better, he was a bargain hunter. With a wife and four children to support on a blue collar salary, it simply made no sense to him to try to grow edibles that could be found cheaper at the store. He did well to keep a small lawn and several spindly trees alive through regular watering.

The only reason Mama ever willingly went outside in New Mexico was to get to the car to go somewhere or to hang clothes out to dry. She always wore a sunbonnet or a headscarf due to the intense sun and constant wind. Though she admired pretty flowers and homegrown vegetables, she had no interest whatsoever in growing them.

When I was a child, my maternal grandmother had a large vegetable plot on her farm in Agee, Texas. It produced most of the produce she and Grandpa needed for the entire year. But by the time we made the 450-mile trip to see them each summer, except for fresh cherry tomatoes, her harvest was in jars in her pantry. Sadly, I did not learn any gardening tips from her either.

Daddy's autistic brother had a large vegetable garden in Gatesville, Texas. Uncle Jay also raised rabbits, which were far more interesting to me and my siblings. But when his older spinster sister would fry one of his bunnies for dinner and Uncle Jay would announce at the table, "This is one of old Spot's young-uns," we were far more interested in eating his vegetables.

We only had one houseplant when I was a child, thanks to me. I vividly remember my very first gardening mistake—Hydroponics.

When I was nine, Mama's sister had the prettiest trailing vine on her kitchen window sill. Its shapely leaves were lime green with red stems and veining. It intrigued me that a sweet potato in water without any soil could grow into a plant. I was convinced Mama just *had* to have one, too. Never mind she didn't want one cluttering up her windowsill, getting in her way at the sink. Though it wasn't easy, I begged until she relented.

It dismayed me that we only had Irish potatoes on hand. Since Daddy bought all of our groceries, I knew if the price wasn't right, he wouldn't buy sweet potatoes. Even if they were on sale, he was too practical to waste good food on anything as frivolous as a houseplant.

I couldn't wait. To make the Irish potato sweeter, I added a pinch of sugar to the fruit jar half-filled with water and secured the tuber with toothpicks so only its lower half was submerged.

Though it took forever, roots and shoots finally sprouted. Because the lone elm tree in our backyard shaded our kitchen window, the tuber received insufficient sunlight. The plant grew tall and spindly, like Jack's beanstalk, and didn't trail a bit. The plain green foliage was boring. Unlike my aunt's beautiful vine, mine was ugly and disappointing, and Mama constantly complained it was in her way.

A sandstorm blew up one afternoon. A strong gust of wind sent my experiment crashing into the sink. The plant was demolished and the root ball would not fit into another jar. Though it devastated me, Mama was overjoyed to be rid of that misfit nuisance. I realized early on that potato tubers, like the green thumbs of mothers,

are not created equally and substituting spuds can result in duds.

It was a visit to the Japanese Sunken Gardens in San Antonio, Texas when I was 12 that got me hooked on gardening. The moment I stepped into that oasis, I was certain I had been catapulted to Glory Land. Though I dreamed of having a beautiful garden of my own some day, it was years before that would happen.

I met my husband at Hardin-Simmons University in Abilene, Texas. Ed's college basketball coaching career saw us moving 15 times the next 25 years. I had numerous houseplants but mainly planted annuals outside since it was doubtful we'd still be around to see perennials come back. It wasn't until we settled in Carrollton, Georgia, in 1993 that I could finally put down serious roots. The results were so gratifying I expanded in all directions. Soon I had more garden than any woman my age could possibly manage.

Ed and I each have our own turf on our sloping lot. He grows vegetables and berries while I concentrate on ornamentals. It's obvious we're not lawn enthusiasts.

In 2002, my garden was featured on Carrollton's Hidden Garden Tour. That same year I achieved certification as a Georgia Master Gardener. Building my garden prior to taking that course, and the fact I am a do-it-yourselfer forever in a hurry governed by one of Ed's possible ancestor's famous laws, made me an expert on gardening mistakes—enough to fill a book. Although it is true, some names were changed and a few liberties were taken in the interest of humor. Some dialogue was also tweaked to assure a PG rating.   *–Shelly H. Murphy*

1 THWARTING CALAMITY

The crusty old driver with scraggly gray whiskers chewing a wad of tobacco stood in our driveway talking to Ed. Parked behind them was a huge grimy *Roy's Septic & Sewer Service* tanker truck.

The man tipped his filthy backwards baseball cap toward me and said, "Howdy, Ma'am. As I was telling your husband, I can't hook up another bathroom to this here septic tank. It ain't big enough to handle it because you already got 2½ bathrooms on it, especially with them old drain lines that could fail any day.

I frowned. "Can't you install a bigger tank with new drain lines?

"No Ma'am, not when there's a sewer you can hook on to. This here city's got rules. They'd fine you and me both for everything we're worth and shut me plumb down if I done that." A wad of crud flew from his grungy mouth and landed near a camellia.

I held my tongue and heaved a sigh. *Tobacco Mosaic Virus, you jerk! Don't you know it can infect every plant it touches?*

"Exactly what does that involve?" I asked, fearing the worst. Our sewer tie-on was in the farthest corner of our odd 1½ acre lot that was shaped like a paper kite in back and piece of pie minus one bite in front. Direct access would involve digging a ditch through our lawn and four terraced perennial beds, a rock path and two more areas filled with prized specimen shrubs, trees and blueberry bushes and then across a dirt road, through a stand of native hardwoods and ultimately over a 15-foot drainage ditch. Not only my garden but our entire property would be devastated, including our largest native oaks! This place would never be the same.

"Well, it's best to just run a sewer pipe downhill in a straight line from here to yonder," he said, pointing toward the cement ogre some 200 feet away that the city installed when they incorporated our subdivision into the city limits 15 years ago. I'd immediately sprayed the obtrusive eyesore brown to help obscure it. "Be lots cheaper that a way, too," he added.

Ed faked a grin. "Exactly how cheap?"

"Oh…about $4,000-$5,000 once you figure everything in." He spit again. "The city charges a big fee to hook on and them big trees down there's real thick— might lose a couple of them."

Exactly how big is your ditch digger?" I asked.

"Pert near wide as a golf cart I reckon."

My stomach churned as I visualized the destruction such a monster would cause cutting a diagonal swath through my garden. Ed heaved a sigh, no doubt relieved that his fenced vegetable plot with raised beds on the northeast side was out of harm's way.

"We'll have to get back to you," I told the man, vowing it would never happen. *You're nuts if you think I'm paying you to devastate my most treasured material possession. Every spare dollar and a dozen years of blood, sweat and tears went into building that garden, ripping out brambles, hauling in and rolling and placing rocks, amending and digging hard red clay to plant hundreds of plants on a slope. That's my paradise where I play and think and pray—it's my therapy. You've no idea how much it means to me.*

Ed put his arm around my shoulders as the man drove away. "Sorry. I know how important your garden is to you. What's for lunch?"

"Whatever you want to fix," I said in disgust. "I've lost my appetite."

Ed munched on a turkey sandwich with the TV blaring as I sat in a stupor staring at the floor. A few minutes later I called the contractor.

"Mr. Davis...I'm sorry, but we've decided not to convert our garage into a new bedroom and bath. It's going to cost more than we ever imagined. That's right. Thanks." I hung up the phone.

Ed's jaw dropped as he frowned at me and pressed the mute button. "Has your mind been fogged by too much fertilizer dust? You know how hard it's getting for us to climb those stairs up to our bedroom with my bum knees and your arthritis. Now we'll have to sell this place and move to assisted living—or give it away in this grim economy. You've been planning this for the past three months. We'll pay for it with IRA's."

"You don't get it, do you? Our gardens are the only reason to keep living here. Besides, we can use what we save on a new downstairs bed and bath to hire help with garden chores until we're both six feet under. For what it costs to hook on to the sewer, we can get one of those automatic stair chairs installed."

"That's brilliant," Ed said, as he leaned back in his recliner and turned up the sound on the television.

2 GOD WILL GET EVEN WITH YOU

From the organ bench I craned my neck to see the beautiful bouquet I'd brought the day before on the communion table in front of the pulpit. My jaw dropped in disbelief as my fingers missed some notes and my foot hit the wrong pedal. All I could see were pathetic withered blooms nestled among greenery! *Did someone knock over the vase and spill all the water after I left yesterday? Was the heat accidentally turned on last night? No, I took the flowers without permission and God is getting even with me.*

After the prelude I opened the bulletin where a line caught my eye: "Today's flowers are given to the glory of God by Mrs. Ed Murphy." I wanted to die.

Averting my eyes from the choir sitting directly across from me, I kept them glued to the music until the song portion of the service ended. When the pastor began his sermon, I slid off the bench onto a folding chair in the corner and stared at the floor.

"Lousy economy," I grumbled to myself. Last year when I'd signed up to furnish flowers the second Sunday in June, I was so confident my newly-acquired degree would land me a good job in accounting that I could order flowers from the florist if necessary. Due to the recession, it hadn't happened. I was still unemployed and money was tight.

There was no florist section in the lone grocery store in our tiny town. Not a single bloom could be found in my yard or my neighbors, mostly soccer moms who worked outside the home. I called several women with reputations for having beautiful gardens, only to learn a late freeze robbed hydrangeas of all blooms and a scourge of Japanese beetles decimated every rose. *It's Friday already—what on earth can I do?*

I thought of Mayzie Fay Green in the country. Two years before she'd had our literary arts club over to see her beautiful daylilies, the first hybrids I'd ever seen. She seemed very generous, serving us lemonade and homemade chocolate chip cookies on her patio. When I admired her summer phlox, she dug up a start for me.

I called but got no answer. Next morning, I tried again to no avail. Figuring she was out in her yard, I grabbed a vase and some scissors and headed over there.

When I didn't see Mayzie Fay's car in her driveway, my heart sank. Though she was gone, I couldn't resist looking in back where her daylilies and other perennials were planted in rows like vegetables. The flowers were even prettier and more abundant than I remembered. The daylilies were every color except blue, and most blooms were six to eight inches in diameter.

When I heard a car pull into her driveway, I was relieved until I saw it was her nosy neighbor. Lila Jennings rolled down her window and yelled, "Mayzie Fay's in Mobile for two weeks, Mrs. Murphy. She asked me to keep an eye on her place."

I walked over to her car. "I couldn't resist stopping to see these gorgeous daylilies."

"Aren't they a sight?" She lowered her voice. "Mayzie Fay will share most of her flowers with you, but not those hybrid daylilies. No sir-ee! They're her pride and joy. She gets them from her sister in Georgia and she wants to be the only one in this neck of the woods that has them. Everybody else has plain orange ditch lilies and that's just the way she likes it. But she loves for folks to look at them, so you enjoy yourself now." Lila backed out and headed toward town.

Haunted by my strict Southern Baptist upbringing, I wrestled with my conscience. *Wonder if she'd mind if I pick a few for a church bouquet?* I could hear Mama warning, as always, "Thou shalt not steal;" "Be sure your sins will find you out;" and "Never take anything that isn't yours—God will get even with you."

Surely a devout Southern Baptist like Mayzie Fay won't mind sharing God's bounty with some staunch Presbyterians. Hardly a soul's going to see them, anyway...unless they're at church tomorrow...then a whole bunch of folks can enjoy them.

I got my scissors and vase from the car and turned on her faucet. Despite my good intentions, guilt flooded my soul like the water filled my vase. Feeling like a thief while praying no one would catch me, I carefully spared new buds by cutting stems with a single bloom. After clipping some baby's breath and asparagus fern for fillers, I jumped into my car and sped home.

Once everything was arranged, I stood back to admire my masterpiece. It was so colorful I didn't use the old large yellow florist bow I had to accentuate it.

That afternoon I crept through the back door to the sanctuary. I set the vase on the table in front of the pulpit, and said, "God forgive me." Then I sat down at the organ and ran through Sunday's music several times.

I didn't hear a word of the pastor's sermon. After the benediction, to avoid further embarrassment, I kept my eyes on the music even though I played the piece by ear. I repeated the postlude until the auditorium completely emptied, then grabbed that pathetic vase and ran to my car with tears streaming down my cheeks.

Two hours later the minister's wife called. After expounding on the beautiful music that morning, she thanked me for being their volunteer organist, like she did every time she saw me. Then she casually mentioned the dreaded subject. "By the way, hon'—those flowers you brought today—were they daylilies by any chance?"

"Yes, they were Mayzie Fay Green's hybrids. They looked gorgeous when I took them up there yesterday afternoon. I can't imagine what happened."

"Honey, that's why they're called *day*lilies. Each bloom only lasts a single day. I wonder why Mayzie Fay didn't tell you to wait 'til this morning to pick them."

I swallowed my pride and gave a full confession. "The Devil made me do it and now God's getting even with me."

She burst out laughing. "Three years ago I did the very same thing—for a wedding. I learned the young couple Ben was marrying the next day couldn't afford any flowers, so I decided to surprise them. Mayzie Fay wasn't home, but since the groom was a new preacher, I justified it would be all right to take them without her permission. Boy, did it ever backfire!"

"At least they got there early enough to remove them ahead of time," I said.

"You'd think. But the couple thought the church ladies furnished them and were too polite to say anything; Ben thought that was all they could afford; and, as usual, I was late. When I slipped in after the bridal march and saw that wilted stolen mess, not only at the altar but in every single window, I wanted to die! Ben wanted to wring my neck. But I lived to tell about it and soon you'll be laughing about it, too. That young preacher and his wife still do every time we see them."

"I already am," I said with a chuckle, promising myself never again to take as much as a seed from anyone else's garden without their permission.

'Strawberry Candy' Daylily

3 THE GREENHOUSE EFFECT

I called Mama at her home in New Mexico to firm up plans for her trip. During the next three weeks she planned to visit three of her children, including me. We all lived in different states.

"Hold on, I can't hear you," she said. "The twins are here so I'm cooking some corn on the cob in the pressure cooker. Let me turn that noisy jiggler down."

Bad as I wanted to see my brothers, I was glad I wasn't there for Sunday dinner. Mama's pressure cooked corn had kernels so tough they'd choke a goat. At least the cobs were tender.

When she came back, I couldn't resist reminding her for the umpteenth time that fresh corn would cook in only eight minutes in a pot of boiling water on the stove. "Folks around here tell you to put the water on to boil before you ever go out to pick it."

"This old fresh corn trucked clear across this desert is so tough, pressure cooking's the only way to get it good done," she said.

"When did you buy it?"

"About two weeks ago at Safeway—but it's been in the refrigerator."

I gave up. "So is everything all set for you to leave on Tuesday?"

"I got my plane ticket and Lucille is taking me to the airport. But I may have to cancel my trip if I can't find anyone to water my houseplants. My neighbors are all going on vacation then, too. I hate to let them die after I've worked so hard keeping them alive." Her voice cracked. "Friends sent me several when your daddy died and the twins gave me some for Mother's Day."

It irritated me that anyone who knew Mama's aversion to horticulture would give her live plants for any occasion, even a death. It surprised me she'd give houseplants a second thought, much less become emotionally attached. Truth be known, Mama was afraid of flying. Though she'd flown twice before, this would be her first time going alone. I could tell she was nervous and looking for any excuse to back out.

"Surely you aren't going to let a half-dozen houseplants keep you from seeing all of your family," I said in disgust. "Don't you want to see Laurie graduate from Vanderbilt?"

"Yes," she said with a sigh. "But I'd sure rather everyone came here to see me."

I thought of a trick I'd used before. We'd moved so often the first 25 years Ed and I were married, I rarely got to know my neighbors well enough to impose upon them to water the scores of houseplants I always kept. At the height of my macramé phase, when I tried to make hangers for every pot, my kids once counted 119.

"Try this, Mama. First, give your plants a thorough soaking. Then let them drain really well. Slip a dry-cleaning bag over each plant, and tie both the top and bottom up real tight. Be sure to move the plants away from the windows out of the hot sun. I've used this method several times when I've gone on trips. Sometimes my plants looked better when I got back than they did before I left. It's the greenhouse effect."

Though she was skeptical, having no other choice, she agreed to try it.

Mama called me when she got back home. "I sure had a good time…but all of my houseplants died."

"They died?"

"Fried like hush puppies! I didn't figure that would work."

"Did you water them well before you left?"

"Yes, I soaked them in the bathtub for an hour."

"I bet you didn't drain them good. Root rot is the number one killer of houseplants."

"There wasn't a drop of water left in the saucers."

"I warned you if you left them in front of the windows that scorching desert sun would fry them through that plastic." Surely this was the culprit.

"I moved them all to the center of the kitchen. I did everything exactly like you told me to and now they're all dead twigs. I knew that wouldn't work."

"Did you tie the clear plastic dry cleaning bags up real tight at the top and bottom?"

"*Clear*? You didn't say to use clear. I never save those flimsy bags from the cleaners. I just used black plastic garbage bags. That's all I could find big enough."

"*Black*? No wonder your plants all died," I said in horror, wondering how anyone raised on a farm wouldn't know live plants could not survive for three weeks in total darkness.

I guess sometimes the gardening gene simply skips a generation. After that we always gave her *fakus ficus*. And silk plants suited Mama just fine.

4 MAKE THAT CALL

Shortly after moving to Carrollton, one Saturday morning I worked like a Trojan pulling weeds and planting groundcover. Two days before, a friend gave me lots of freshly-dug vinca minor that needed planting soon. My new neighbor and I had already discussed our mutual dismay at all the weeds under the trees between our driveways. I hoped these new plants would eventually choke them out. While the neighbors were away with their young son in the hospital, I thought it would be nice to surprise them. Boy, did I ever.

After lunch, heavy clouds formed overhead, the wind picked up and it began to sprinkle. I was so desperate I ran inside and begged Ed to come help me. "Tape that and watch it tonight without commercials," I pleaded, knowing it would take a tornado to tear him away from a baseball game.

"Can't this wait 'til next week when the World Series is over?" He grumbled.

"No, this stuff won't last inside these plastic bags. Have you any idea what tiny pots of groundcover cost? This was free, but it's got to be planted today. Rain's on the way tonight and all of next week, which will help get it established. I cancelled my appointment at the beauty shop today to plant it, but I can't get it done without help. Hurry!"

He gave my filthy, disheveled self the once over and said, "Good. That'll give you more time to go to several beauty shops—get at least three estimates!" I wiped my sweaty brow and stuck my tongue out at him.

Begrudgingly, Ed set the recorder, got up from the sofa, lumbered out to the yard and picked up a shovel.

"Just dig small holes staggered every six or eight inches," I said. "I'll come behind you, put in a plug, and cover it with good dirt from this tub. With any luck, the rain will water it for us."

A few minutes later he muttered, "I'm going to the basement and get the pick. This packed red clay's nearly as hard as your head."

The rain held off and we were making good progress when he stopped digging and said, "Shoot! This stubborn root I hacked in two is an electric cable. I bet I cut our telephone line!"

I heaved a sigh of disgust and went inside to check. The phone, TV and lights were all working. When I came out and told him it must have been a piece of old buried wire, we both breathed a sigh of relief.

It was almost dark when the last plug was installed. Large raindrops began pelting our heads and thunder rumbled in the distance. We grabbed our tools and ran for cover.

We were eating supper when our neighbor called to tell us they'd just brought their son home from the hospital. "By the way, is your TV working? It looks like our cable has gone out, right when I planned to watch the World Series."

Ed winced. "Dang! We were out planting groundcover between our driveways today. I bet that stubborn root I hacked in two was your TV cable. I can't tell you how sorry I am. I've got today's game taped. Come over here and watch it with me."

"No thanks, that's O.K. We're exhausted and need to turn in early," he said.

Ed slammed down the phone. "I feel terrible! I can't believe *their* TV cable was buried a whole two inches deep in *our* yard!"

It was the following Thursday before the new cable was installed, since they had to wait until the other utilities got marked. By then, the World Series was over. Ed insisted on paying for it, but our neighbor claimed they didn't charge him. "That old cable never was worth a hoot," he said, "so you did us a big favor."

The only thing worse than cutting your own TV cable in the middle of the World Series, is severing that of your new neighbors. At least we learned the importance of having utilities marked before digging.

In subsequent years it really hit home that damage to buried utilities is not only expensive, but dangerous, when a local woman ruptured a gas line while merely planting tulip bulbs in her yard. The next year a road construction crew erroneously blasted a newly-restored century-old residence in a nearby city to smithereens. If the wire Ed cut had been our home's main electricity line, he could have been electrocuted.

Now I always call 811 before digging, since marking utilities is a free service that is typically done in three to four working days. Otherwise, I might soon be calling 911—if I'm able.

5 IMPUL$E $HOPPING

When I heard Ed's brakes screech in our driveway, I grabbed my purse and ran out the door. "Hurry, bring your pickup and help me load a river birch clump I saw this morning. It's too big for my car." I climbed into the cab beside him.

"Should we call for a police escort?"

"We don't have time. It's got three trunks and it's only $13.95. Oh, *please*, let it be there. It's the last one."

Thankfully, we weren't stopped for speeding. Once we had it loaded on a cart, I breathed a sigh of relief. As we headed toward the cashier, Ed said, "Look—these peach trees are only $10.00. I love peaches. Let's plant one in back where the tornado took out all of those loblolly pines."

"You need two to cross-pollinate or else they won't make any fruit." I checked the tag to make sure it was free-stone and saw it was self-pollinating.

"Get two anyway," Ed said, in keeping with his belief that if one is good, more are better. Once we got them loaded, our cart was full.

"Go get another cart, Shelly. Here's a nectarine tree for $13.00! They're even better than peaches and Bryan loves them. And look—a Bartlett pear for $15.00. And a red plum—it's a little small, but only nine bucks. Is that grapes behind you there? You know they're my favorite." He went around the aisle and checked the tag. "These are only $5.00, so let's get six." Next to the grapes were some thornless blackberries. "Let's get four; they're only $3.99! I love blackberry cobbler."

Ed saw me coming with a second cart. "You won't believe it—I just found an apple tree! We had two in our backyard in Syracuse when I was growing up."

I frowned. "Isn't it too hot to grow apples here? I'm the only one who eats them anyway."

"Why else would they have them for sale? These are 'Delicious.' Isn't that the kind you like? Did you ever see apple trees in bloom? They are gorgeous."

"Once—in the Sacramento Mountains in New Mexico. They were pretty."

Ed smiled. "Our backyard will look terrific with all this stuff blooming the same time as the dogwoods."

I shook my head. *In several years we'll need a fruit stand at the end of our driveway.*

My cart's wheel caught on some bare root four-foot twigs by the fence. "These redbuds are only $8.00, Ed. Remember how pretty those were in the Texas hill country on the way to that dude ranch? Let's plant one out front. These aren't exactly the picture of health, but everything's guaranteed for a year. I also want one of those tulip trees with pink blooms as big as your fist in back by the fence."

"Those are beautiful," Ed said. "I'll get one and meet you at the register."

"No, I want to pick it out to make sure it's the right color and has a pretty shape." On the way to the back I passed by a pink dogwood. At $35.95 it was no bargain, but I couldn't resist. A clerk saw me and brought an extra cart. After loading it and a $40.00 Japanese magnolia, he rolled them to the front. Ed was parked near the door with his treasures loaded when I finished checking out.

"Good grief, Shelly. It'll take us a week to get all this stuff in the ground."

On the way home, I cringed at the credit card receipts totaling 15 times more than I intended to spend. *Next time, I'll leave Ed at home and get a clerk to help me load my stuff into his pick-up.*

A search for spots to plant our unintentional orchard revealed we had a problem. The sunniest part of our yard was overtaken with wild blackberries. By the time we got everything planted among those treacherous thorns, we looked like we'd fought a pack of rabid hyenas and they'd won.

Sparse rain fell that year. Dragging a hose through that tangle of brambles to water every week convinced me it was wild blackberries that surrounded Sleeping Beauty's castle, allowing her to sleep undisturbed for 100 years.

Fast-forward 15 years for a progress report. The Bartlett pear tree was spindly and never had a single bloom. After learning that particular variety neither thrives nor bears fruit in our area, I secretly chopped it down the fifth year to make room for a hammock.

The red plum tree was white. Though it grew quite large and had pretty blossoms in early spring, its fruit was always rotten. Ed never took advantage of that brief window of opportunity to spray the blossoms to prevent the dreaded curculio worm attack on fruit trees in the South every spring. One day I hacked it down on impulse because it deprived our blueberry bushes of necessary sunshine to bear fruit. Though it upset Ed, he got over it. The nectarine tree fell victim to these same culprits. After struggling a few years, it met its waterloo when a septic tank cleaner annihilated half its roots.

One peach tree died of natural causes in its fourth year so I planted a weeping Yoshino cherry. The other one's fate is the subject of another chapter.

The apple tree lived longest of the large fruits under the canopy of towering native trees. Its handful of blooms bore no fruit. The tree succumbed either to the drought of 2006-2008 or to Cedar Apple Rust, a disease which occurs when cedar and apple trees are planted in close proximity. The two topiaries south of my gazebo some 15 yards away are red cedars. Since most of Bryan's pets liked to eat apples, he buried two hamsters, his favorite beagle, and a gecko under that tree. At least it served as a unique grave marker for a time.

As for the small fruits, we enjoyed fresh blackberries until the deer discovered them and soon they were history. Once the blueberries got sufficient sunlight, they did well with little care. The Concord grapes steadily declined until they died. We learned too late they dislike intense heat and humidity, and must be sprayed five or six times a year. Native varieties like muscadine and scuppernong grapes do better here.

The pink dogwood struggled along a dozen years. In dense shade from the outset, it had few blooms and its leaves were perpetually coated with powdery mildew. We later learned pink dogwoods just don't do as well as white ones in this county. The year after we had total outdoor water bans, it bit the dust.

The redbud tree out front has grown unusually large. When in bloom, it's delightful. But its branches droop to the ground and over the driveway and require pruning. It is unattractive when loaded with brown seed pods. Since the trees aren't long-lived, I'm taking the stance "let it be." Quite by coincidence, the 1995 bombing of the federal building in Oklahoma by Timothy

McVeigh occurred right after I planted it. The redbud is Oklahoma's state tree, and folks were urged to plant them as memorials to souls lost in that tragedy.

The Japanese magnolia out front is still alive and gets gorgeous pink blooms every year. But it typically happens too early and late freezes often blitz them. In fact, a former neighbor used to predict the next freeze would occur the day after that tree was in its glory. Sadly, she was usually right.

My once-prized river birch clump surpassed all expectations. Now over 70 feet tall, its ominous branches arch in all directions, shading half my circular bed of Knockout roses and other sun-loving perennials. It not only saps moisture from the azaleas and ferns beneath it, but our Bermuda sod has died out due to its dense shade. Though its peeling bark is attractive, especially in winter, each spring an infestation of worms strips its branches bare. The slightest breeze causes it to drop limbs everywhere and I'm weary of picking them up. I learned too late these trees are short-lived and are also susceptible to storm damage. My dream is to replace this mistake with an attractive Japanese maple.

These days when shopping for plants, first I make sure there's a good spot to plant them, especially trees. I also no longer assume that if a retailer has a plant in stock it will flourish here. This not only spares numerous problems, but also saves me money.

Unlike Ed, I've also learned to forego special kits for growing tomatoes upside down, as well as the latest speedy-weedy gizmo, and battery-operated owls to deter wildlife (or most anything that requires batteries). Armed with proper knowledge and a good deal of effort, I hope to afford gardening as long as I wish.

6 TOO MUCH ALREADY

When someone asks to see your garden and you always tell them, "Sure...but wait until June," you've probably planted too much of the same thing. In my case, it's too many June bloomers like daylilies and hydrangeas. But by then the annuals planted in April look good. The St. John's wort is bathed in golden blossoms. The roses, not to be outdone, are also showy. Ditto for the cannas, gardenias and even the mums. It seems every blooming thing peaks simultaneously. Except for annuals like zinnias and impatiens, and perennials such as phlox, salvia and black-eyed Susans, the other summer months are comparatively drab.

Good garden design calls for a succession of blooms throughout the year. This takes careful planning and experimenting. Even then, bloom time is not a sure thing, since temperatures and moisture are also factors.

About the only time my daylilies were not in bloom by the first week in June was the year my brother and his wife from Abilene, Texas, came to see us. They had never seen hybrid daylilies before, and I wanted them to see mine so badly. But a late spring freeze caused everything to suffer a setback. The daylilies didn't bloom until about June 10, after they'd gone home, and the hydrangeas didn't bloom at all that year.

The first year Ed began a vegetable garden in Alabama, he grew 47 cabbages from seed. No telling how large his first crop would have been had he not thinned out the seedlings. Back then our family of four consumed about three cabbages per year: one boiled with a ham hock in mid-winter; a second with corned beef on St. Patrick's Day; and a third in coleslaw for the Fourth of

July picnic. Cabbage is best eaten fresh since it cannot be canned or frozen successfully. We had no desire to engage in the tedious, smelly process of making sauerkraut, which we liked but seldom ate. And we lived in a very small town.

Ed immediately gave a cabbage to each of our neighbors. He took several to the university to give to colleagues. That weekend he loaded them into his pick-up and gave them to friends around town. But he still had 32 left.

While preparing to cook the first one, I noticed the leaves were riddled with tiny holes. When I cut it open and saw some velvety green dudes moving like inchworms, I called Ed to take a look.

"Yuk—your cabbage is full of worms!"

He shrugged. "Big deal. It's got the added bonus of a little protein—a complete meal in a pot!"

"You need to give the rest to a pig farmer," I said, tossing it into the trash.

It embarrassed me the next week when I learned Ed again tried to give wormy cabbages to everyone he knew. "Don't tell me they all took another one," I said.

"Some did. Not everyone's as persnickety as you when it comes to eating a few critters. Did you know the USA is the only country in the world that doesn't eat insects? Well, we do—but not on purpose. They're ground up in flour and stuff so nobody notices."

I sighed. "Just compost the rest."

During the next two weeks, though Ed offered a cabbage to almost everyone he met, there were few takers. One wife complained there hadn't been that much gas in one place since a pipeline ruptured. It wasn't until Ed realized folks were avoiding him, even running away whenever they saw him coming bearing cabbages that he gave up and tilled the rest under.

Despite my complaints, every year Ed plants more vegetables than we can use, although he rarely has to sneak up on friends' front porches at night to unload them. Most Southerners will gladly take fresh produce, especially tomatoes. For years he took extras to his office. Now that he's retired, it's harder to give away things like this year's bumper crop of scorching hot peppers. Luckily, the Latino chef at a local restaurant took them and made a tasty five-alarm salsa verde.

Ed realizes he shouldn't grow more cucumbers or zucchini than he can use or give to folks and still manage to keep them as friends. I know not to plant so much of one thing that it's boring, or so many varieties my landscape looks too busy and helter-skelter. I try to use enough of the same plants to give my yard cohesion and interest in several seasons. Depending on the size, groups of odd numbers look best and have more impact.

7 PEACHES OR POND

My giant intimidating husband stood on the deck watching me in the yard below trying to dig. He frowned at me and boomed, "Put that goldfish pond anywhere you please...but don't you dare touch my peach tree."

I looked up at him and scowled. Resuming a contorted stance, I pushed my foot against the shovel with all my might. It was no use. The compacted Georgia red clay was full of stones and hard as granite, just like his head. It was impossible to dig that area out to fit my rigid pond form at an angle. When I tried to stand up, my straw hat snagged on a branch and fell off.

"Cursed peach tree," I grumbled, jamming my hat back on. I wanted to kick myself. Why I ever enlisted Ed's help in bringing home a river birch clump was beyond me. I should have known he'd come back with a ton of plants we didn't have room for or need, just like this crummy peach tree.

"We have 1½ acres here, Shelly. Don't tell me you can't find another spot for your pond."

"How about smack dab in the middle of your vegetable patch?" I snarled. "Would that make you happy? That's exactly what the experts recommend—in full sun on level ground away from trees." Ed made no comment and went inside the house.

I wanted my goldfish pond and waterfall on that slope in full view of the deck so bad I could hardly stand it. That some spindly $10.00 peach tree would keep me from it was unbelievable. Especially one that hadn't grown a foot in three years, and the one time it had blossoms, all three got zapped by an early freeze.

After putting my tools in the basement, I slammed the door and marched up the stairs to the family room. Ed was plopped on the sofa with the TV remote in his hand. I glared at him and said, "Just load that pond form in your pick-up tomorrow and take it back for a refund." Near tears, my voice cracked. "We just won't have a fish pond. It's impossible to dig it out with that darn peach tree in the way."

"Settle down, Shelly. Wait 'til this weekend and I'll help you dig it. I'm sure we can work around one little peach tree."

For certain that would never happen, with college basketball games on TV and heavy rains in the weekend forecast. Besides, the tree would forever be dropping leaves and rotten fruit into the pond, provided it didn't croak. Its roots would all be forced to grow on one side, restricted by the pond and waterfall liners on the other. It wouldn't work. That tree had to go. We not only had another one exactly like it across the yard that was self-pollinating, we also had nectarine, plum, apple and pear trees, plus blackberries, strawberries, blueberries and grapes. How much fruit could a family of three eat with a mother who never made jelly?

Two weeks later, I was lying awake nights trying to figure out how to get rid of that tree and still keep my marriage intact. I'd learned years ago that it was easier to beg Ed's forgiveness than to ask his permission. It made me furious that I hadn't secretly chopped it down in the first place. Given his acute dyslexia, he likely never would have even noticed.

One sleepless night it occurred to me that George Washington, an honorable man and one of our nation's founding gardeners, had chopped down a cherry tree in his youth and lived to tell about it. Why couldn't I, an honorable middle-aged woman and future Georgia Master Gardener, do the same to a lousy peach tree? I could even buy Ed another one if necessary. Armed with new resolve, I couldn't wait 'til morning, when he was leaving town for a three-day meeting in Birmingham.

I got up at 6:00 a.m. and did some chores inside. As soon as Ed pulled out of the driveway, I ran to the basement and got the hand saw. Two minutes later, the deed was done. I carried the spindly peach tree deep into the woods to hide the evidence. After marking out the area, I got busy wielding my pick and shovel. Recent rains had softened the hard red clay a bit, and the weather was cool, cloudy and pleasant. It wasn't as hard to dig as I anticipated.

By the time our son, Bryan came home from school that afternoon, the pond was completely roughed out. During the next two days, after making sure it was level, I added sand. I not only got the rigid pond liner completely installed, but also dug out the long waterfall and put the liner in it. It was amazing what I had accomplished. Now the project only lacked rocks, water, pumps, filters, plants and fish.

When Ed got home and stepped out onto the deck, I braced myself for the worst. He leaned over the rail, looked over my new project and said, "Wow, is that neat! I can't believe you put that pond in while I was gone. I was sure I'd have to dig it for you when I got back." He turned and gave me a high five. "Way to go Hon'—it's beautiful!" We both breathed a sigh of relief.

Sooner or later the inevitable will happen. One afternoon from my kitchen window I saw Ed on the deck looking down at my pond. All at once he put his hands on his hips and said, "I cannot believe that nervy woman chopped down my peach tree!"

When he marched inside the kitchen, I beat him to the draw. "That peach tree must have been real important to you. It took a whole three weeks for you to notice it was missing. Shall I buy and plant you another one, Sweetheart?"

He shook his head and swallowed his words. Then he came over and hugged me.

Photo by Richard Anderson

8 DOOM AND HOOTIE

"What a mess this place is!" I muttered to myself.
"How will I ever get it shaped up in time? When will I
ever learn to just say 'No'"?

In a moment of weakness the day before, I'd
agreed to let the daughter of a friend's best friend have
her senior pictures made by a pro in my garden today at
3:00 o'clock. There were weeds to pull, flowers to
deadhead, vines to tie up, lilies to stake and paths to
sweep. Moreover, the lawn needed mowing and the
blueberries were ready to pick.

July's heat was intense and I was hot and thirsty. In
my haste to get started that morning, I forgot to take my
usual ice water with me. When I saw the blue thermos jug
from the day before was still on the table under the deck, I
was relieved. After taking a big swig of the lukewarm
liquid, I grabbed my rake and a plastic tub to tackle the
chore I resent most.

Ed feeds birds year-round in my garden. I'm
convinced these feathered friends, totally dependent on
his welfare support from the moment they leave the nest,
could not possibly survive on their own in the wild. Early
on he devised a system using ropes and pulleys to raise
his feeders high up in the dogwood tree near our house.
Since it was the most technological feat he ever
accomplished, it impressed me. It allows him to watch
wild creatures from his favorite spot on the family room
sofa and also from the deck. The system also makes it
convenient to lower his feeders for refilling.

Ed keeps a tube feeder filled with thistle to attract
goldfinches; a block of suet for the red-headed
woodpeckers; and a squirrel-proof feeder full of black oil

sunflower seeds to attract cardinals and blue jays. After he noticed the pesky rodents were having difficulty obtaining food from this latest gizmo designed to keep them out, Ed felt sorry for them. He installed another pulley system in the sweet gum tree by the deck with a wire holder for dried corn on the cob specifically for them. In his words, "I find the squirrels are often more entertaining than the birds." This is certainly the case when they do acrobatic feats in order to obtain sunflower seeds from his squirrel-proof feeder, which they manage to do quite successfully.

From the outset, this smorgasbord has been a bone of contention between us. Although I also enjoy watching birds, I detest the unsightly mess they make. Each week a bushel full of seed hulls collects and litters the rock path and what's left of the lawn beneath the dogwood. When it rains, these hulls wash into my flowerbeds and seeds sprout here and there occasionally. Since rumor has it the black oil sunflower seed hulls will kill every plant they touch—although I haven't noticed any casualties yet—it infuriates me that Ed refuses to clean them up. He claims this natural debris is just like mulch and perfectly harmless, the exact same excuse he uses for not helping me clean up the tons of leaves that collect on our pathetic front lawn every fall.

Raking furiously, I was tempted to teach Ed a lesson by mulching his vegetables with the tubful of hulls I'd collected. I was getting sweatier and madder by the minute at getting stuck with his chore, when I saw something strange flopping under the deck. Since I hadn't taken time to put in my contact lenses that morning, I squinted to get a better look.

Our 12 year old happened by so I grabbed him by the arm. "Go see what's flopping under the deck."

Bryan ran up there and yelled, "Oh no—it's Hootie!"

"*Hootie!*" I said in disbelief. Surely it wasn't my outstanding Shubunkin that was white with vivid orange and black spots. *How did a fish manage to escape from my smallest pond and travel 40 feet away?* Our black stub-tail cat was sitting nearby looking guilty. "I bet Doom caught him and took him up there. How bad is Hootie hurt?"

"I think he's O.K. but he's panting hard and has dirt all over him," Bryan said.

"Hurry and get that new blue bucket out of the basement and fill it up with water from the pond. And while you're there, see if the Blowfish is O.K. We'll isolate Hootie in the bucket for awhile to make sure he's all right before we put him back into the pond." I had serious doubts my favorite calico fish would survive.

I couldn't imagine Doom's latest shenanigan. Bad enough that cat continuously annihilated vermin, but this time he'd gone too far. I wondered now why I'd let Bryan keep the stray, especially since we were all allergic to him. Besides, his hunting habits were disgusting. The week before, while sitting on the basement stairs putting on my shoes, a putrid odor hit me. I looked down to see a dead male cardinal right beside my foot. On two occasions, I'd performed mercy killings on frogs with missing hind legs near my ponds. I'd also spotted several lizards minus tails scurrying across paths. Once Doom even deposited the remains of a dead chipmunk inside my garden shoe by the step. At least he kept our mice problem in check—there hadn't been one in the basement in months.

Turning my attention back to my chores, I frantically swept paths, snipped off yellowed leaves and deadheaded blooms. The sun was so hot it made me sick to my stomach and my head throbbed. Despite the fact a migraine headache seemed imminent, I kept working. From time to time I took a swig of water from the blue thermos jug on the table under the deck, even though it was warm and tasted dreadful.

Just before lunch I decided to check on Hootie. When I didn't see the blue bucket anywhere, I went to see if Bryan had tossed him back into the pond. The Blowfish was swimming around, but my prettiest fish was nowhere in sight. *What has that child done with Hootie?*

I went inside and began calling neighbors to try and find him. Four calls later, Bryan was on the line.

"I couldn't find that new blue bucket in the basement, Mama, so I just put Hootie in that blue thermos jug of water on the table under the deck."

I dropped the receiver, made a mad dash for the bathroom, and threw up.

9 FROM DEVASTATION...AN OASIS

The evening my local Master Gardener group came to see my garden, most all of my plants were at peak of bloom. Recent rains made everything extra lush.

As members entered, I told them, "We have three rules in this garden: watch your step; stay on the paths; and if you see a weed—pull it!"

"What did this backyard look like before you built this garden?" Mary Lou asked.

"You wouldn't believe it. Sixteen years ago when we bought this place it looked like a war zone back here." I explained how in November of 1992, a tornado swept down and toppled every loblolly pine to the ground in this backyard and those of several neighbors. It was a miracle none of the towering giants fell on the houses. Though the other neighbors cleaned up their yards immediately, this place was being rented at the time and the absentee owners didn't bother.

In retrospect it's likely the reason they accepted our low offer in July of 1993. We were on our way to look at a house across town a final time before buying it, when our realtor got a call these owners were desperate to sell. We agreed to come take a look.

Though only four years old, the home's white siding needed painting. The front flowerbeds were overrun with weeds six feet tall and weeds were even growing in the gutters. Although the walls and bath tiles were nondescript beige, the carpet was ubiquitous purple raspberry. Despite its flaws, we liked it. Unlike other homes in our price range, it was large enough for our furniture. It also had a full basement, a first for us. We loved the privacy the spacious wooded lot afforded on a cul-de-sac in a quiet park-like neighborhood. There were lots of native hardwoods and numerous rocks of all sizes. We had moved enough times to know fresh paint, new carpet and lots of elbow grease would soon have the place back in shape. With judicious pruning and weeding plus lots of TLC the front yard could be restored. We were both foolish enough to take on the challenge in the back.

As soon as we closed and moved in, we were lucky to find a pulp wood hauler to take the downed loblolly pines in exchange for the wood. After loading seven truckloads, breaking several saw blades and chains, and battling a pesky hornet's nest, by week's end he surely had second thoughts. We gave him several more precariously-leaning pines after our new next door neighbor told us, "There are basically two kinds of loblollies: the kind that are going to fall on your house this year in a storm and the kind that are going to fall on it next year." He also donated several by his house.

We hired a man with a front-end loader to clean up the debris, level off our backyard as best he could and still leave the native hardwoods intact. He spent two days loading branches onto a truck and pushing huge stumps deemed too cumbersome and expensive to haul away into a far corner. Given the numerous times he struck big rocks, he must have been cursing. I wondered what we'd ever do with all those boulders he unearthed. Ed told him to scoop up all the good dirt and dump it on the bare flat area on the northeast side for his future vegetable plot. Rye grass was planted to prevent erosion.

I turned my attention to unpacking boxes and getting my household settled. The backyard would have to wait. Like Miss Scarlett in *Gone with the Wind*, I decided to worry about that tomorrow. It amused me that after residing in Georgia only a few days, I'd assumed the stance of its most famous heroine.

The following spring Ed planted his vegetable garden. Ruff, Bryan's beagle puppy, dug so many holes our backyard looked like Prairie Dog Town. Over the next two years, wild blackberries and weeds overtook the rest of the area. We fought our way through those wretched thorns to water all of the fruit trees Ed bought on impulse.

In 1997, Bermuda sod was installed near the house in back and I made a border for flowers. Beyond that, our large lot sloped downward so the plan was to leave that area wild and natural. Trouble was, I couldn't see my new bed from my kitchen window and had to step out onto the deck. Plus those pernicious wild blackberries were hazardous to children and pets that regularly cut through there on their way to the creek in the woods. In self defense, that fall and winter I donned protective clothing and declared a one-woman war on those brier thugs. By spring not a single wild blackberry could be found in that area. Although I didn't know it at the time, this cleared the way for my ornamental garden.

Since I also wanted a goldfish pond with a waterfall, I decided to build it on the right side of the slope, and put three more terraced beds for perennials on the left. That way, I could enjoy my flowers and pond from my kitchen window. Ed was delighted with the top-rated tiller I gave him for Christmas, never suspecting my ulterior motives. He was clueless that come spring, he'd be tilling halfway to the Newnan Highway. I got so excited about designing and building new flowerbeds that, like the Energizer Bunny, I simply couldn't stop. Before I knew it, my garden was larger than I ever dreamed.

My flowerbeds were held in place with stacks of smaller rocks from our yard. I outlined paths with medium-sized stones and saved larger ones for my proposed rock garden around a waterfall and small pond. Naturally, there weren't enough rocks, so searching for them at a construction site in Ed's pick-up turned into regular family outings. The rocks were unloaded at the top of the slope, and then I rolled the heavier ones into place to build my waterfall and surrounding rock garden. Though "Rolling Stones" is a rock group to most, it was my primary pastime for several years.

Naturally, the first pond I installed with a rigid liner was too small for the koi I thought we wanted. The next year I built a larger pond below it with a flexible liner and then connected the two with a waterfall. I learned too late the second pond was also too small for fish that got so large. To date the consequence of having two smaller ponds and falls instead of one huge one has been double the trouble and expense.

In 2001, I purchased 12,000 pounds of flat field stones. I used some to edge the ponds, and fit and leveled the rest for paths in jigsaw fashion over a bed of crushed gravel. A mixture of dry concrete and sand was swept between the stones and misted with water to set it. This worked all right for flat areas, but after rains caused washout on the slopes, I had to mix up concrete to redo paths in several areas. I also used it to build five stone steps on the sloped path leading to a small central patio.

Since my favorite color is rainbow and my favorite pattern is paisley, for a time whenever a new plant caught by eye, I took it home and found a spot for it later. Then I promptly forgot what was planted where or what color the blooms were until it was too late. This resulted in a cottage-style, anything goes, garden. At first I planted whatever I could get my hands on—like my children, I loved them all. But through the years a good many plants have fallen out of favor with me and I've become more selective.

Will I ever get it completed? Of course not. Since change is the only constant, a garden is never finished. There is always something to be redone, added or removed. My friend Becky claims "A garden is a job forever." And she's right.

10 IRONY IN ACTION

Meshach and Abednego were easy to capture, but Shadrach gave me fits. Feisty and cautious, the goldfish was determined to escape the green devil that snatched his cohorts. It took numerous futile attempts before I nabbed him. In my haste to be done forever with that nasty 15-gallon aquarium at the far end of my kitchen counter, I failed to keep a firm hand over the green net. Shadrach flipped out and landed in a corner, panting heavily, doomed to die. I cringed as I swooped up the slimy creature with my bare hands and plopped him into the pail with the others.

I marched down the deck stairs and flung them into my largest pond, much like their Biblical namesakes were cast into the fiery furnace. After cleaning the aquarium a final time, it was relegated to the basement pending my next garage sale. I was ecstatic that after five long years our aquarium saga had ended. It was hard to believe my child agreed to move them outside.

By the time Bryan came home from school, his aquatic pets were thrilled with their new-found freedom. Zipping from side to side and top to bottom, even a 12 year old could see they loved their spacious new habitat. Though it occurred to me goldfish that old might not survive the winter, at least they'd spend their final days happy. Besides, they had the whole summer to adjust.

From the outset, that aquarium spelled disaster. What I never realized, after agreeing to let Bryan spend his allowance on a $10.00 tank, is all the extras needed to make it like the store display: colored gravel; a scenic background; assorted aerating plants; a decorative treasure chest; ph kit; thermometer; pump; both under gravel and outside filters; fluorescent light and bulbs—a plethora of parts sold separately that broke down the day after purchasing costly replacement fish and amphibians with short life spans that were incompatible. Bryan was traumatized when Winky, his $5.00 waterdog, devoured Kermit, his tiny $12.00 albino frog, the very first night. It also upset him when his new bettas, Samson and Delilah, tried to kill one another had we not moved one to solitary confinement in the nick of time once we realized all red ones aren't females and all blue ones aren't males as a friend led him to believe. That I'd finally convinced my child to stock his aquarium with a dozen cheap goldfish was a triumph in itself. During the last two years, these three lone survivors grew large.

To my surprise, the goldfish did survive their first winter outdoors, despite harsh weather, including snow. They hibernated quite well under a large black plastic crate held down by a huge pot of hardy water lilies. We kept the pond from freezing over by placing a mini-basketball in the water to bobble up and down.

In spring the trio could be seen near the top searching for food. Bryan checked the pond thermometer daily, anxious to supplement their diet of mosquito larva and algae with purchased pellets once the water reached 55 degrees. Soon they were coming to him like little puppies to be fed and even petted.

One day I made the mistake of letting "he who thinks if a few are good then more are better" take his son to the pet shop to buy crickets to feed his gecko. To my horror, they came home with 20 feeder goldfish.

"We decided Shadrach, Meshach and Abednego could use some company," Bryan said, his eyes gleaming. Nothing thrilled him more than the prospect of some new pets. "Dad agrees with me that a big pond like this needs more fish."

I glared at Ed. Before I could warn Bryan to leave the new fish in their bag in the pond for 30 minutes so the temperature would adjust, he had opened it and dumped them in.

To our surprise, the Goliath threesome scurried over to a corner, terrified by the David-with-slingshot-like invaders. After hovering there for several minutes, Shadrach, Meshach and Abednego disappeared under the crate. By dark, they were still in hiding, letting the little ones have the run of the pond. We were amused.

Next morning before school, Bryan went outside to check on his pets. A minute later, he screamed so loud I ran out onto the deck to see how badly he was hurt.

"Mama, come quick! He wailed, as tears streamed down his cheeks. "The big fish are attacking the little fish! I only see two still alive. Hurry, come help me rescue them."

I ran to the basement for the net and pail. By the time we dipped the dead ones out and caught the five remaining live ones, Bryan had missed his bus.

In the car on the way to school, he turned to me and said, "Promise me you'll get the aquarium back out today, Mama. We've got to keep those little fish on the kitchen countertop until they get bigger."

My heart sank and a lump formed in my throat. *Dear God, what did I do to deserve this?*

11 WHAT'S IN A NAME?

Upon hearing that I had registered for the Master Gardener course, a friend said, "I've always wanted to take that course too, but I'm too lazy to learn the Latin names for every plant on the planet."

What have I gotten myself into now? The last thing I want to do at my age is learn names for a gazillion plants in a foreign language. I only want to learn more about growing plants in general, and to share that knowledge with others as a volunteer.

It relieved me to find the course did not require learning the botanical name for every plant. Based on past experience, though, you'd think I would have learned years ago the importance of knowing proper botanical names for plants.

After Ed landed his first head-coaching job in Alabama, we left Kansas as soon as school was out. Our Chevy sedan was loaded to the brim for the 625-mile trip. Our tall, skinny kids who were 10 and 13, sat in back separated by a bird cage housing a lone finch named Archie. (Edith, his mate, succumbed the month before leaving no progeny, due to her disgusting habit of laying her eggs while perched in the swing.) Duffy, our nervous Cock-a-peke, whose severe under bite with protruding eye teeth earned him the nickname "Vampire Dog," took turns sitting on their laps. The trunk was crammed full of valuables, photos, and keepsakes, plus enough belongings to last us the estimated five days until our moving van arrived. (We ended up spending ten agonizing days at the town's only inn—the place really put the "eek" in economy lodging.)

Several nice houseplants I couldn't bear to part with took up every spare inch inside the car, forcing us to sit in our appointed spaces like we were positioned for MRI's. A spider plant with prolific offspring was situated between Ed and me in front. A robust philodendron trailing six feet long wound around between my feet. Hanging baskets of Swedish ivy, wandering Jew, and asparagus fern in the rear window tickled the kids' necks. I figured this inconvenience was a small price to pay, considering the cost to replace them. It was the late seventies and I was smack dab in the middle of my macramé phase. All those hangers I'd made needed plants.

Having lived the previous 12 years in the desert Southwest and Kansas plains, we were taken aback by the lush terrain the further south we drove. As we rounded curves in low places overtaken by gigantic vines sporting huge leaves, all the kids could say was "Wow." As darkness ensued, the moonlight trickling through towering trees—smothered by what we'd later learn was kudzu, the weed that ate the South—formed silhouettes like scary monsters waiting to pounce.

We couldn't wait to live in Alabama. When we'd been there in early April for the job interview, we were in absolute awe of the spring landscape. In sharp contrast to the bleak windy days in Kansas, it was Mecca. Dogwoods, spring bulbs and azaleas were blooming everywhere. We adored the small trees still barren of leaves covered with gorgeous fuchsia blossoms resembling giant tulips. Folks in Alabama called them "tulip trees," a name which seemed altogether fitting.

Several years later in the fall of 1986, when Ed landed the head men's basketball coaching job at Ole

Miss in Oxford, Mississippi, we bought a brand new house under construction with a large barren front yard. It was February before we could finally move in. As soon as we got unpacked and settled, we rushed to a local nursery to buy a tulip tree. I'd heard the best time to plant trees is late winter while they're still dormant and I was determined to do it right (I would learn later that fall is best for planting trees in the South). This tree would be the focal point of our front yard, surrounded with azaleas and cheerful bulbs in spring, colorful annuals in summer, mums and asters in fall, and pansies and ornamental kale throughout winter. Our yard would surely be the envy of the entire subdivision.

When I asked the nurseryman for a tulip tree, it surprised me when he frowned and said, "Might be one in back somewhere—we don't get many calls for them."

"Don't they do well here?" I was almost certain I'd seen several around town last fall.

"Oh, they do quite well," he assured me before he disappeared to the back.

I rolled my eyes at Ed, wondering why the man wouldn't keep a supply of these beauties on hand.

The owner emerged a few minutes later carrying a six-foot-tall barren stick with several lateral branches in a five-gallon pot of loose dirt. It looked like he'd just dug it up. When he said it cost $15.00, my heart leaped since I expected to pay two or three times that much. We also bought some compost and mulch he recommended and headed home for the planting.

Despite the fact my tulip tree did not have a single bloom the first two years, it looked healthy and grew unusually tall. I figured it wasn't mature enough to bloom. Frankly, I hadn't given it much thought. Duties like looking after Ed's terminally-ill aunt her last six months, plus helping our daughter who'd just graduated from Vanderbilt University get settled in her first teaching job and own apartment, complicated by my newborn son, prevented me from completing the plantings around my focal point tree. The simultaneous demands of helping a fledgling leave the nest while hatching a new one had made a tired old bird out of me.

One warm spring day I was standing in the driveway watching my rambunctious toddler flit around the yard like a hummingbird on speed when my next door neighbor came over to chat, as she often did.

Suddenly she pointed at my focal point tree and said, "Look...your tulip poplar is blooming."

My jaw dropped. It was covered with *yellow* blooms nestled among leaves!

Then she pointed at our woods in back and said, "I noticed last week all your wild tulip poplars were blooming. Now the one you planted out front is too."

I was flabbergasted. No wonder my tulip tree grew so tall and never had pink blooms.

There was no way I'd admit to her or anyone else that I'd wasted good money trying to make a focal point out of a weed tree. I took a deep breath, faked a big grin and said in my best southern drawl, "Well I declare. It sure is...I thought it never would...isn't it *pretty?*"

The best thing about moving four years later was leaving that particular mistake behind. At least I learned that the only way to assure getting an exact plant is to know its proper botanical or Latin name. Colloquial names for plants vary from place to place which is why some experts only use proper names in book indexes and mention common names only in plant descriptions.

Even then, plants can be mislabeled and tags can accidentally get switched or lost. They can also have different characteristics due to being another cultivar of the original plant. After seeing 'Bluebird' Hydrangeas in a state botanical garden and two private ones, I knew mine got mislabeled at some point. It may be 'Lilacina,' but I can't be positive. However, I prefer mine over most 'Bluebirds' I have seen. Whatever it is, it pleases me and that's really all that matters. (I have since purchased a genuine 'Bluebird'.)

I know now the best time to buy a plant that blooms is when it is blooming. The "what you see is what you get" rule applies here. Whenever I don't know a plant's Latin name, I try to at least give a detailed description. Had I only mentioned to the nurseryman that the tulip tree I wanted had *pink* blooms as large as your fist, surely he would have sold me a Japanese magnolia; not a native tulip poplar.

12 MAKE IT GOOD, FAST & CHEAP

Shortly after I completed the Master Gardener course, a young woman who had seen my garden on Carrollton's Hidden Garden Tour the previous month called me. Now that she and her husband were settled in their first new home, she wanted me to come over and advise them what to plant in their yard.

Despite my newly-acquired gardening expertise and years of learning through mistakes, I felt incompetent for the task. However, since I didn't want to disappoint her and knew this home visit would count toward the 50 volunteer hours required to become a certified Master Gardener, I agreed to come take a look.

Though her homebuilder had installed Bermuda sod in her front yard, she wasn't pleased with the tiny shrubs around her front porch. Her main concern was her huge backyard, which was fairly typical of the rolling hills in central Piedmont Georgia: hard red clay with knee-high weeds in full sun. The sole tree on her property was a large dead one in back of the lot, which she didn't want to bother removing. She also wanted to screen a back corner to hide an offensive orange house in the distance.

I learned that she and her husband both held demanding jobs, had two young children and generally disliked yard work. They didn't own a shovel or a hoe but thought there might be a hose somewhere. She looked me right in the eye and said, "I just want it to look really pretty as soon as possible and I don't want to spend much money."

I excused myself to the powder room and looked into the mirror to see if I might have turned into the Fairy

Garden Mother. If only a beautiful yard could be had *good, fast* and *cheap* with merely the flick of a wand. Unfortunately, one can choose any two of these, but never all three, for several reasons:

If it's good and fast, it won't be cheap. My friend called a reputable landscape company who helped her decide what she wanted. Then they brought in a crew and installed it in a jiffy. However, it took a second mortgage to pay for her new checkbook landscape.

If it's fast and cheap, it won't be good. When we first moved to Georgia, I was so anxious to have a pretty yard I didn't do my homework. The first thing I did was buy plants on impulse at a discount store. The fact I had to buy a pick to dig the first planting hole confirmed my suspicion the soil was unusually lousy. I'd heard somewhere that sand would help make hard red clay soil more porous. So Ed tilled in several bags of sand with native soil for my first perennial bed. I realized too late that sand plus clay plus water plus heat makes bricks! Needless to say, my new perennials were not happy, as evidenced by their speedy decline and ultimate demise. So I had to start over and amend the soil with aged pine bark, which cost me even more time, labor and money.

If it's cheap and good, it won't be fast. If I had it to do over, I would first seek professional advice. Garden designers often charge by the hour to come up with a plan for a plot. They will determine individual needs, assess terrain, sunlight, soil and drainage issues; plan irrigation, guest parking, paths, and retaining walls; and recommend the best plants for specific areas. Then a homeowner can work on small areas of the landscape plan as time, energy and budget allow. Since a little knowledge goes a long way, I realize now this would have been the wisest money I ever spent and would have saved me in the long run.

I advised the young couple to have their back lawn installed by professionals, since they would likely never get it done themselves. I suggested planting trees next, since the best time to plant a tree was 20 years ago and the second best time is today. Trees also increase a property's value. Two large deciduous oaks or maples at least 25 feet from the house in back would shade the offensive west sun on their patio and kitchen window in summer and allow sunlight in to help reduce heating costs in winter. A Japanese maple or a spring flowering tree would add interest and be the ideal size for their front yard. A staggered group of tall pyramidal evergreens like Japanese cryptomeria would screen the rear of their property. Several large lightweight decorative pots for colorful seasonal annuals on their front porch and rear patio would suffice since I deemed flowerbeds too labor-intensive for them.

They followed my advice, and seemed pleased with the results. Though I offered to provide plans for curved perennial beds around their yard they could add when their children were older and they had more time, they weren't interested. A few years later, the young family sold that house and moved away.

13 GENUINE R & R

The first three years we lived in Carrollton, each fall we made a day trip to the mountains in north Georgia to see the leaves. While we saw lovely waterfalls and beautiful scenery, we had no luck finding color at its peak. Steep winding roads, an irritable youngster, disagreements on where to eat, how often to stop, and what radio channel to choose, had us asking one another at several points, "Are we having fun yet?"

After one such exhausting trip, Ed and I were sitting on our deck trying to unwind just before sunset. I looked at all the trees surrounding our property and said, "This is the best fall color we've seen all day." He agreed. The red sumac and evergreens mingled with the glorious shades of gold, tan, rust and orange of native trees comprised an outstanding palette. Needless to say, we haven't made a fall trip to those mountains since.

Now I've been married to a full-blooded Irishman long enough to know that all too often one gets the urge to go see what's over the hill, or at least the nearest state line. But such trips are often a far cry from the genuine rest and relaxation we crave. All the fuss and bother of getting ready, coupled with traffic snarls, crowds, high fuel prices or long security lines and inconveniences, can leave one utterly exhausted. Several of our weekend getaways left us wishing we'd rented a room at the nearest rest home instead.

What's the solution to some genuine *R*est and *R*elaxation? We built a private oasis right in our own backyard. Now we can sit down and unwind whenever we wish. It's a project we did together that provided plenty of good wholesome exercise and tangible results.

I'll admit I've never worked so hard in my entire life. In retrospect, I wouldn't advise anyone my age to tackle a project as large as mine turned out to be without hiring some help. Since I did most of it before I became a Master Gardener, I made so many mistakes I now regard them as my primary area of gardening expertise. Creating the garden is one of the more gratifying things I've ever done, however. It has brought me and my family more enjoyment than we ever imagined. The best thing about it is that we can take a short staycation any time we wish.

Since a garden is never finished, it will always be a lot of work and some expense. But the rewards make it all worthwhile. It's a great way for me to vent my frustrations and Ed claims it's cheaper than a psychiatrist. He loves to unwind after a hard day's work in his favorite spot beside the waterfalls under the canopy of an oak tree, where he can watch the birds feed, or take a break from working in his vegetable plot. We frequently drink coffee and read the morning paper there when the weather's nice. Bryan and his friends are also fond of the garden, especially all the critters it attracts like squirrels, birds, deer, frogs, lizards, turtles, snakes, insects and once even a stray black cat with stub tail destined for quick adoption. Merely stepping into the garden full of Mother Nature's wonderful sights, sounds and smells, invokes a peaceful, relaxing feeling for every visitor.

A backyard oasis doesn't have to be huge or elaborate. Perhaps the best thing about gardening is that almost anyone can garden almost anywhere. It only needs to be comfortable and pleasing to the owner. A couple of comfortable lawn chairs under a tree or an umbrella on a deck with several pots of colorful flowers may suffice. Birdbaths and feeders will attract wildlife to observe. A small inexpensive fountain can provide the relaxing sound of water. To me, the main object is to make it serene.

If I had it to do over, I would make my garden lower-maintenance. I know now how important it is not to take on more than I can handle, and not overdo to the point I spend half my gardening budget on painkillers and chiropractors. Gardening is a hobby. The purpose of a garden is to please. Above all, it should be fun.

14 GARDENING'S ROUGH WITHOUT RUFF

We gave the cutest beagle puppy you ever saw to our five year old for Christmas. With eyes gleaming, Bryan announced, "I'm naming him Ruff—so he can say his own name." It was love at first sight. Soon the two were inseparable, romping and playing like brothers. Bryan claimed Ruff was the best present he ever got.

For me, it was the worst. I realized too late that Ruff had one *huge* flaw: his nose and brain were the same organ. An overpowering sense of smell ruled everything that stubborn hound ever did—he was basically a nose with four legs. He escaped at every opportunity and wouldn't come when we called him. He barked incessantly, as he relentlessly chased cats and wild critters into the woods behind our house. At four months, one day Ruff treed himself when he chased a squirrel to the tip of a precariously-leaning pine; after barking so long he was hoarse, Ed had to take a flashlight and ladder to rescue him. The pooch dug so many holes our backyard resembled giant honeycomb. He chewed a huge hole in the back of an armchair and destroyed all three beds I bought him on the very first day. After spending all day outdoors, whenever Bryan brought him inside, Ruff would sneak upstairs and mark his territory on the carpet. No amount of calling, threats, coaxing, treats, or even an occasional beating would make that ornery beast mind. The scourge of the neighborhood, Ruff was misery disguised as a pet.

Ed and Bryan loved him; I didn't even like him. I spent sleepless nights trying to figure out ways to rid myself of Santa's mistake and get my life back to normal.

I promised myself that the very next day I would drag that hound from hell right back to the kennel from whence he came and demand a refund—or maybe even pay them to take him back. I would secretly place an ad in the paper, "Free beagle to a good home; call only during school hours." Or I would sneak off early with Ruff in tow and leave him at a pound so far away he could never be rescued in time. One Christmas I almost bought a stone engraved "Beloved Pet" just in case we might need it. (*They don't routinely necropsy dead dogs, do they?*) But somehow I could never manage to carry out any of my plots. Though the scoundrel was the bane of my existence, Ed and Bryan would never forgive me if they ever found out. While Ed claimed Ruff kept varmints out of his vegetables and also my flowers, I was convinced this horrible hound was useless to me and even hazardous to my health.

When Ruff was four, Ed accidentally ran over him in our driveway at noon one day. Fearing the pooch would surely die, he agonized over how he could ever tell Bryan when he got home from school that he'd killed his best friend. I, too, feigned great sorrow, as I turned aside and whispered "Thank you, God." At last—divine intervention! I was terribly sad and hated to see any animal suffering, but hey—Que sera sera!

But it was not to be. Ruff not only didn't die, he never even missed a meal. The vet said his pelvis was broken and the ordeal did sideline him for awhile. But all too soon he was back in action, up to his same old tricks. He was never quite the same, however. He limped slightly, ran slower, slept more, grew fatter, and lived for several more excruciating years.

It's true one never realizes what something is worth until it's gone. Within a week after Ruff finally died of natural causes, I noticed a rabbit nibbling in my garden. Some groundcover was mysteriously missing the next day. By summer, the deer were having a heyday, even at mid-day, defiantly crunching Ed's vegetables. By fall, they were devouring my hostas and azaleas. After planting my pansies in October, next morning half were missing and the rest were devastated by deer tracks. My neighbor, admittedly no fan of Ruff, said her pansies were eaten right out of their six-packs on her porch and her hostas disappeared. She just could not understand it because she'd never had a deer problem before. When I told her it was because Ruff was gone, she assumed a deer-in-the-headlights stare, obviously in shock that a sorry nuisance like him had worth to her, after years of antagonizing her cats.

Did we ever replace Ruff? Despite my protests, Ed tried. Clementine was the cutest beagle puppy you ever saw. A better canine for our cul-de-sac, she even minds occasionally. Ed and Bryan love her and...well, so do I. But I realized too late, Clementine has one *huge* flaw: her defective nose makes her a disgrace to her breed. An indoor lap dog, she prefers barking at strangers and chasing stuffed animals to wild varmints.

Now rabbits and deer feast freely in our garden. Squirrels feed daily at our bird feeders. The neighborhood cats are at peace. Some things, like good garden dogs, simply cannot be replaced.

15 I DON'T DO BUGS

The woman on the phone sounded so frantic I wondered why she wasn't calling 911.

"Help! Tell me what to spray on these roses a friend gave me—they're covered with bugs! I'm hosting a bridal shower tomorrow and want to use them for a centerpiece. Now I don't know what to do-o!"

"What do the bugs look like?" I asked.

"Hundreds of tiny light green creepy crawlers! They send cold chills down my spine."

Though I was tempted to give my normal response regarding insects: "I don't do bugs—I just let them do each other," it appeared the culprits were aphids.

"Try this trick. Take a hose with a nozzle and put it on a light spray setting. See if you can't gently wash the bugs away. Normally you can take a hose and blast insects off your flowers before you pick them, but roses are so fragile they might fall apart."

"*Water?*" I could tell she was shocked.

"Yes, plain ordinary tap water. It will be safer for the refreshments on your table and your roses won't smell like nasty bug spray. Did you know that only 3% of bugs found in the garden are harmful? The other 97% are good guys that pollinate plants and feed birds and other wildlife. Those bugs on your roses are aphids, the primary source of food for ladybugs."

"Well I never knew that," she said. "Thanks, that'll save me a trip to town to buy bug spray."

Given that so few insects found in a garden are harmful to plants, it is easy to see why indiscriminate spraying of pesticides can do more harm than good.

Ed and I are fortunate. The lots in our subdivision are large and back up to the woods, so we are relatively isolated. The fact our close neighbors don't have vegetable gardens allows us to use less harmful pesticides only as a last measure of defense, like Bt, a naturally occurring soil bacterium. Many times when vegetable gardens are in close proximity and one or two gardeners are avid pesticide users, others in the vicinity develop infestations and are forced to use pesticides, too.

When we first moved to Georgia we had fire ants. Periodically, our neighbor called an exterminator to poison those on his side of the island of trees between our yards. Almost overnight, new mounds appeared on our side. I tried various methods like pouring boiling water down the hole and using a shovel to destroy the mound and expose the eggs, and they would disappear. Soon my neighbor would have the exterminator back.

For several years the fire ants seemed to move back and forth between our yards. Then at some point, they disappeared. No doubt my neighbor thought the bug man's smelly milky solution finally worked. But the fire ant mounds in my backyard also vanished, and poison was not used on them. Rumor had it some virus might be destroying fire ants, like the honey bees that are growing scarcer. But after learning that ingesting corn meal can also wipe them out, I wondered if the corn meal based pre-emergent I used to deter weeds in my flowerbeds might have been a factor. Whatever caused their demise, it's great they're gone.

In June each year when Japanese beetles start devouring my roses, I don plastic gloves and vent my frustrations by flicking them into a milk jug with some warm soapy water. Sometimes I rub the devastated bloom and beetles between my hands to destroy them.

In the late nineties when bug bag traps were all the rage, I put one smack dab in a circle of tea roses. It was both disgusting and gratifying to watch those bags fill up with Japanese beetles and then discard them into the garbage. But the next year, the infestation was ten times worse than the year before. When I realized the remedy was attracting additional Japanese beetles from a widespread area to my yard that were laying tons of eggs before they dropped into the bag, I stopped using it. No doubt the best results with this method can be obtained by placing the bags several houses down the street in the yard of an irritating neighbor.

A friend claims a sure way to get rid of Japanese beetles is to first borrow a bagful from a neighbor. Add a little water and pour them into a blender (you'll also want to borrow your neighbor's blender). Grind the beetles up well and spray the mixture on your plants. I haven't tried this, but he vows you won't see any more of the culprits. Despite their faults they're not cannibals.

I also pick off harmful varieties of caterpillars by hand. For smaller insects, I spray both sides of the leaves with insecticidal soap. I also use this on houseplants that spend the summer outdoors before bringing them inside for the winter.

Ed's first attempt at growing strawberries was a disaster. Each morning he found the ripening fruit devastated by unknown culprits. It wasn't until he gave up and ripped out his plants that he saw the underside of an old cracked bleacher board he used as a walkway between his strawberries was covered with slimy slugs.

Most folks know the best remedy for slugs is to put a saucer of beer beside the plants. The slugs will crawl into it and drown. I tried this with my hostas once but it backfired—have you ever seen a tipsy beagle?

Tiny green worms on the underside of leaves riddle my perennial hibiscus full of holes as fine lace. Despite this perpetual abuse, the plant reappears every year. Though I've tried to ignore the pests in hopes some natural predator might wipe them out, next year I'm using garlic spray. If that fails I'll use a botanical pesticide, which also kills Japanese beetles.

Indiscriminate spraying of insecticides may kill the bad bugs but will also get the good guys like praying mantis, lady bugs, lacewings, honey bees and beneficial wasps. These insects are our pollinators, so vital to the plant fertilization process, including the produce we eat. Many caterpillars morph into those beautiful butterflies we all enjoy. Insects also feed wild birds, lizards and frogs. Even the detested fire ant eats termites. The jury is still out on the pesky mosquito's merit except to feed bats and Purple Martins and to drive human beings mad.

Native plants and herbs will help attract beneficial insects to a garden. These dandy dudes can also be bought over the internet and shipped in a dormant state, ready for release into the garden. I'm mindful though, that once they consume whatever's bugging me, they may leave my place in search of more.

Some bugs may appear to be good guys at first. When the state Master Gardener office sent out an e-mail alert about a kudzu-eating pest, I viewed it as cause for celebration. At last, a natural remedy. Folks have tried to banish this Japanese groundcover thug intent on overtaking the South since it was first introduced in the 1870's. (A self-proclaimed Whiskeypalian in Alabama claimed "the best way to get rid of kudzu is to spray it with bourbon—the Baptists will gnaw it to the ground!") Unfortunately, I was wrong. The kudzu bug, a native of India and China, also likes soybeans, a major U.S. crop vital to both animals and humans throughout the world. First sighted in Wisconsin in 2000, within two years it had spread to crops in Georgia. It's obvious this evil bug must be controlled since it is also fond of green beans.

When I had tea roses (and hence a good many aphids) ladybugs were prolific in my garden. Every fall they would flock inside and congregate on my ceiling, seeking refuge from the cold. For several years I put a nylon footie over my vacuum cleaner nozzle and sucked them up. Then I reversed the suction and splayed them into my attic for the winter. These days I don't see many ladybugs. Whether this is because I no longer have tea roses or due to the trauma my vacuum cleaner caused them remains a mystery.

Companion planting, or combining certain herbs and flowers with vegetables works well to repel insects, although I've yet to convince Ed to try it. He's so paranoid I'm trying to take over his vegetable plot for my ornamentals that he refuses.

On those rare occasions when one must resort to using insecticides, there is an all-natural pesticide made from chrysanthemums that helps control ants, bedbugs, fleas, lice, roaches, silverfish and ticks. Strong mouthwash sprayed into the air deters mosquitoes from an outdoor gathering. A sheet of fabric softener in one's pocket will also help keep these pests at bay.

I try to seek earth-friendly solutions that are deemed least harmful, using commercial pesticides only as a last resort. It's easier and cheaper just to let the bugs do their thing and let nature take its course. We are all better off in the long run.

16 WINTER INTEREST

One frigid February evening I was sipping hot tea at my kitchen table piled high with plant catalogs and gardening books. I was drawing up a blueprint of my five-year-old garden when Ed interrupted me.

"What are you doing—dreaming up new ways to spend my hard-earned money?"

"I'm trying to add some year-round interest to my garden. It's so boring in winter with everything dead."

"So tack a laminated poster of Raquel Welch in a bikini to the oak near where I sit."

"You're dating yourself, plus all that air-brushing would make it too expensive."

"Then put one of Angelina Jolie in a bikini and Brad Pitt wearin' a speedo!"

I sighed. "I'm talking about year-round color."

"Surround 'em with a flock of pink flamingos!"

I giggled and waved him away.

For me, winter is the longest season of the year, followed closely by scorching hot summers, while spring and fall seem to fly by in fast-forward mode. How often I've bemoaned the short span of time the dogwoods and azaleas bloom, and that all-too-brief period of fall splendor. It always saddens and depresses me the morning after the first killing frost to know my garden will be dead and ugly the next several months.

If only I'd had the foresight to plant more evergreens in the first place, now I wouldn't be facing this dilemma. Adding plants at this stage would mean rearranging, perhaps even banishing established perennials. But something had to be done. I could not endure another depressing winter.

Several evergreens already grew in my garden. Seedlings of Lenten Rose planted last year were coming along on the shady slope among my hostas. Talk about slow growers—no wonder they're so pricey in nurseries. The cast iron plant under a native tulip poplar was looking good. The variegated winter daphne my garden club gave me when Mama died was not only thriving, but perfuming my entire winter garden. The mahonia by the deck surpassed all expectations in height and its yellow finger-like blooms were also fragrant. Hybrid azaleas, autumn joy sedum, lamb's ear, daylilies, St. John's wort and gold mound spirea also looked good throughout milder winters. An Indian Hawthorne by the deck stairs had nice foliage, but voracious deer typically devoured all spring blooms.

My new plan added several evergreen shrubs in the rear: sasanqua and Japonica camellias, pink azaleas, a leucothoe, a loropetalum, and a gold thread-leaf false cypress near the hammock. It also called for a red rhododendron and three boxwoods by paths in the pond area around the table and chairs. Several nandina 'Firepower' scattered throughout the terraced beds would add year-round appeal as would two upright red cedars shaped into three pompons across from the Rebecca statue. Four Confederate jasmines would intertwine with large-flowered purple clematis at each of the arbor's four posts. Variegated Japanese aucuba in various spots would give spark to an otherwise bland landscape and then fade into the background as spring bloomers steal the show. A Japanese pieris 'Mountain Fire' would be a great addition since late winter flowers from buds resembling strings of tiny beads would be followed by fiery red new growth in spring.

To me, the best thing about a winter garden is that its hardscape or "bones" are so prevalent—stones, paths, walls, arbors, benches, statuary, water features and evergreens all contribute, only to be somewhat obscured by "flesh" of foliage and blooms in spring.

Wildlife is easier to spot without competition of foliage. By regularly providing seeds and suet, we attract beautiful birds. This same food appeals to squirrels and raccoons, which are also entertaining. I usually leave the foliage on dried grasses as well as hydrangea and echinacea blooms for winter appeal. The latter also provides food for birds.

Wind rustling through dried matter adds yet another dimension of sound to the winter landscape. The river birch's bark, though interesting year-round, is more noticeable then. Interesting patterns of contorted barren tree branches are intriguing on cold dreary days against the backdrop of a changing winter sky. Stunning sunrises and sunsets are more prominent that time of year, and savored by the appreciative eye. For color, pots filled with hardy annuals like ornamental kale, chard, violas and pansies are most attractive in mild winters. Frosts on gardens lend winter interest and snow can turn them overnight into winter wonderlands. The fact it rarely snows here makes it not only inconvenient but extra special.

Though I always dread the approach of winter, and rue that morning each year when I awake to find most of my garden shriveled beyond recollection, I'm mindful that gardening in the tropics could get boring. It's akin to a Christmas poinsettia that lasts until May—I get so tired of it by March I want to toss it out. Change is not only inevitable, but good. I'm trying to accept, if not enjoy, winter for the role it plays. That brevity of splendor each season affords is the reason I've learned to appreciate each one while it lasts and to look forward to the next one so much. The four seasons are simply part of God's greater plan.

Despite his best attributes, the best part about ole man winter for me is yet to come—kissing him goodbye.

17 WHOSE TEAM ARE YOU ON?

I glanced at the clock–7:30 already, barely enough time to dress and get to the Ag Center by 8:00. As Corresponding Secretary of Master Gardeners, I was responsible for the monthly newsletter and could not miss a board meeting. I'd spent too much time that morning browsing through a new plant catalog.

With a towel wrapped around me, I was drying my hair when I remembered the outside door to the basement was still locked. I forgot to tell Ed to open it before he left for work. The air conditioner repairman was coming at 9:00 that morning. The day before, I discovered a large puddle of water on the basement floor around the water heater. I waited half the day for a plumber, only to learn the leak was in the air conditioner pump beside it. The bogus service call cost me $65.00.

I rummaged through my drawer for my favorite beige undies and remembered they were all downstairs in the dryer. Gardening every spare minute from dawn to dusk caused the laundry to pile up for over two weeks. I reached in back and grabbed an ancient black lace bra and matching panties and put them on. Then I threw on a pink fleece robe and darted downstairs.

A musty odor assaulted me the minute I opened the door, reminding me why I always warn repairmen to enter our basement at their own risk. To further mask my embarrassment at its deplorable condition, I always tell them, "I keep the house, but this basement's my husband's domain—it's his job to keep it neat and tidy."

The mere thought of all the grit and grime on the basement floor made me cringe. I spotted Ed's size 15 high-top basketball sneakers on the second step and slipped them on my bare feet. Clinging to the rail, I lumbered down the stairs and rounded the corner.

It looked like the set of a Stephen King horror movie. I flicked the light switch but it would not come on. There was too much junk underneath it to get a ladder in to change the four eight-foot fluorescent bulbs.

Praying I wouldn't stumble in the dim light and hurt myself, I stepped across a big pile of old gardening shoes and cautiously made my way through the narrow path toward the door. Our chest freezer, three gallons of water, two coolers, a metal plant stand, and a water heater were on my right. To the left were stacks of empty boxes, cans of paint and supplies, an antique bench and two wooden rockers with worn-out seats, four sets of stained green cushions, a torn wicker hamper, a broken vacuum and microwave awaiting the annual electronics recycling event, three aquariums, old bird and hamster cages, and several bags of cat food and litter. I dodged assorted gardening tools leaning against the crude monster tool holder that Ed built from two-by-fours and vinyl lattice.

I made my way around three rolls of soaker hose, stacks of newspapers, assorted black pots, bags of composted manure, a can overrun with trash, and four five-gallon buckets. Everything was covered with spider webs, dirt and debris. Now the floor was a muddy mess. *Will I ever find time to clean up this nightmare?*

While maneuvering around a metal garbage can full of black coated sunflower seed for wild birds, the loose string of Ed's left clodhopper caught on a reel wound with orange electric cord attached to a leaf blower. I stumbled and fell against the door.

I unlocked the padlock, removed the heavy security chain, and flung it open. Fresh spring air and singing birds made me long to be working outside. *How*

Shelly H. Murphy

do they always manage to schedule meetings on the most gorgeous days? Rain's predicted the next three days and throughout the weekend. At this rate, I'll never get my garden shaped up this year.

When I turned around for the venture back upstairs, I saw water spraying from the ceiling. *Not another leak!*

Too nearsighted without my contact lenses to pinpoint the problem, I squinted and spotted the step ladder in a web-infested corner. In order to reach it, I moved aside a giant tiller; a lawnmower; a fertilizer spreader; two bicycles; a wheelbarrow; a rattan swivel chair used for sitting out tornado warnings; a monster Bryan made in art class from two-by-fours, rubber hose and a Swahili mask; a fake Christmas tree wrapped in an old sheet beside three boxes of decorations; and a wooden coffee table sporting a bloody stain left by a bird our cat brought inside to kill.

As I made my way back through the maze of junk carrying the ladder, I grabbed Bryan's blue football helmet and put it on to keep my hair from getting wet. I moved aside three 40 lb. bags of composted manure and several stacks of black pots to set it up.

My foot was on the first rung when a hot flash hit me. About to melt, I stripped off my winter robe and tossed it over a rake handle. Though the spewing water soaked my undies, it was refreshing and cooled me off.

Halfway up the ladder it was obvious the copper tubing leading through the floor to our icemaker directly upstairs had sprung a leak. Luckily, a cut-off handle temporarily solved the problem.

I had just started down the ladder, when I glanced up and could not believe my eyes. Standing in the doorway was a well-built young man in a blue uniform with a tool box in his hand—the air conditioner repairman was over an hour early!

I sailed off that ladder, landed in a squat, flung my arms around myself and froze! Even without my contact lenses, I could tell his eyeballs were as big as Park's Whoppers, and knew my face was just as red.

Rendered speechless for a moment, he pondered the menopausal marvel hunkered down in a mud slick of the messiest basement on the planet outfitted in a football helmet, drenching wet black lace undies and Bozo the clown sneakers.

He cleared his throat, tipped his cap toward me and said, "Gosh, I sure hope your team wins today, Ma'am."

18 START WITH A PLAN

I held my breath and watched with extreme angst as a guest who likely weighed over 350 pounds tried to sit in a flimsy plastic chair. In a bind to provide extra seating for Ed's annual get-together at peak time in my garden, the chair was one of six I bought on sale for $8.00 each. The tags indicated a 200-pound weight limit.

Since Ed is 6' 7" tall and weighs 285 pounds, I had already cautioned him not to use them. So offering to exchange seats with this man was not an option, not that Ed was paying the slightest bit of attention. *Why doesn't one of these thinner guys here today offer him one of the sturdy steel patio chairs they're sitting in?*

Influenced by Irish solutions, these members of the Steering Committee prided themselves as solvers of world problems. They typically met at one of the local pubs every Friday, but a favorite spot was the dining set on the dinky patio beside my ponds and waterfalls.

The annual get-together was growing by leaps and bounds. Men had started bringing their wives and kids along. Today there were already 15 guests gathered around the table under the canopy of an oak tree. It was filled with appetizers I'd spent most of the day preparing and cold drinks were in a cooler beside it.

A very pregnant wife maneuvered her way through the crowd and sat down beside me on a stone step. *I can't believe these men won't offer their seat to her, not even her own husband.*

The arms of the chair caught on the heavy man's backside. *Oh no—he's stuck!* Turning red, he managed to wriggle loose from its grip and stood behind Ed.

I jumped up and offered him my spot, but he indicated he was fine. The step was so low he might not be able to get back up. *Why doesn't one of these munchkins take the hint and switch chairs with him?* He had some refreshments and then made some excuse and left. No doubt his feet and back were killing him.

After the party ended, I scolded Ed. "Why didn't you be a good host and offer him your sturdy chair?"

"Because he wouldn't take my seat—I'm nearly twice as old and overweight, too. Besides, calling attention to his weight in a crowd would embarrass him."

I never dreamed when I built this garden that anyone other than my family and a few friends would gather on this patio or I would have tried to make it larger, although space was naturally limited by trees and topography. It turned out to be such an irresistible central and shady spot for enjoying the garden and waterfalls that no one ever wanted to sit elsewhere.

My garden has other design flaws, as well. Its cottage style on a slope is not in keeping with my formal Georgian-style home. One of the most important elements of garden design is building one that fits its surroundings using compatible materials, which means I should have used bricks instead of rocks. Never mind I couldn't afford brick paths and walls, which means my garden would not have happened.

To me, formal design requires flat terrain and large square grassy areas surrounded by hedges and duplication in quadrants. However, I prefer free-flowing curves with a variety of plants in groups of three or more. Being something of a Willa Rogers (I never met a plant I didn't initially like) too much repetition of plants would bore me. Had I the means to bring in tons of dirt and build a lengthy retaining wall in order to level my sloping lot, I not only would have lost almost every native tree, I would have hated it. Though at first it was disappointing, I soon realized being on a slope lends another dimension to the space, almost a 3-D effect.

To compensate for its casual style, I installed a couple of formal areas, like the statue of Rebecca at the Well under my wrought-iron gazebo, which is my garden's primary focal point. There is also a statue of the famous bird girl in John Berendt's book, *Midnight in the Garden of Good and Evil,* on a tall pedestal in a circular bed of Knockout roses surrounded by lawn.

Another key element in garden design is to get the proportions right. Here again, I failed miserably. Scale can be tricky outside where everything looks smaller. I know now my rock paths are too narrow; the gazebo is too close to a weeping cherry; a river birch clump is rivaling a cell phone tower; and a red Japanese maple is too close to the deer fence surrounding Ed's garden, although the tree was there first.

I have learned to compensate for several design flaws. This past June when we again hosted Ed's Steering Committee and other friends, I placed the drink cooler by the table near the falls where the men always congregate. The food was served inside our screened porch, where the women and children took advantage of a ceiling fan's breeze and comfortable seating free of insects. Last May, to avoid gridlock around the table by the ponds and to accommodate aging members when my garden club came, we sat in lawn chairs on the grassy area and served refreshments on the patio under the deck. Guests avoided stairs altogether by walking around the other side where a moss-covered slope gently curves around terraced beds of hydrangeas.

I realize now the faux pas in my yarden are a designer's nightmare (one visitor jokingly called it an "interesting conglomeration of semi-controlled chaos"). My front yard is shamefully neglected and drainage is still an issue; lighting is insufficient; the lack of planned irrigation makes watering a huge chore; handicap access is non-existent; some areas are not as safe as they need to be—handrails by the stone steps would be helpful; one large pond would have been better and cost less than two smaller ones that serve as further proof that two wrongs don't make a right. Also, my plant selection is too hodge-podge; I've created more than I can maintain; and the list of blunders is endless.

In spite of its flaws, kind friends and relatives have told me it's the prettiest garden they've ever visited that was done by a novice with no outside help. But the important thing is that it pleases me, and that's really all that matters. Like my home, my garden is simply a way to express myself—my ideas, my style, my space. Hopefully, any visiting designers and subsequent owners of this property will say, "Bless her heart. She did the best she could with what she had."

19 IT SURE BEATS A SHRINK

While riding on a garden tour bus one day, I overheard an impeccably dressed, sophisticated woman say in her best southern drawl, "I just *love* to get out and *dig* in the *dirt*! It makes me feel *so good!*" It took me by surprise, since my first impression was that she was one of those flower-arranging garden club ladies with designer fingernails who uses hired help and would never think of working outdoors.

However, it made me stop and ponder: exactly what is it that compels humans to directly connect with Mother Earth? Is it because life began in a garden? Is it that the fruits of the garden sustain us throughout our lives on earth? Is it because our physical bodies return to dust once our life on earth is over? I concluded it is all of these things—a direct connection; a complete dependency; a vital part of what we essentially are.

In Pearl Buck's Pulitzer Prize-winning novel, *The Good Earth*, the protagonist, even after attaining considerable wealth, would ultimately return to his farm land when things got tough. Gathering up some earth and holding it between his fingers made Wang Lung feel content and able to forget his problems for a time.

I first became aware of the therapeutic effects of gardening years ago in Mississippi. We had just bought, completely painted, and moved a few miles from Cleveland to a house in Merigold. Only 18 days later, I was still unpacking boxes when Ed landed a better job in Oxford, some 90 miles away. This meant yet another house to sell and our 14th move during the past 23 years. Ed left immediately to assume his new duties and our kids went off to college.

One crisp fall day, I was home alone working at a frenzied pace, trying to spiff up the disheveled yard to get this latest house ready to sell. I was totally engrossed in digging out monkey grass that had overtaken the front flowerbeds, when a new (soon to be former) neighbor called out from her yard, "You remind me of Mother. She used to get out and dig to 'vent her frustrations,' she'd say." I realized it was true. I was extremely frustrated, and digging helped me deal with it all.

Though our founding fathers, particularly Washington and Jefferson, knew all about the beneficial aspects of gardening, there is a renewed awareness present in today's society. Universities offer degrees in horticulture therapy. After years of relying solely on prescription drugs for therapy, the medical community is now adding "healing gardens" to rehab facilities. Gardening has proven to be beneficial to autistic children and to Alzheimer's patients, as well. Nursing homes are putting in handicap-accessible gardens. Ghetto neighborhoods in large cities have reserved spaces from razed buildings for community gardens. Even prisons have gardens, not only to help feed, but to rehabilitate inmates. Ed claims that for me, gardening is cheaper than a shrink.

Gardening offers a connection to the past and hope for the future. It promotes camaraderie and interaction among citizens to help combat isolation, loneliness and depression. It increases mental function and memory. Growing food encourages healthier eating and provides necessary exercise. Truly gardens do feed the mind, body, and soul. They are retreats for relaxing and enjoying the sights, smells, and sounds of nature. They are respites from the hectic lives we live today.

Garden author Eleanor Perenyi, who predicted in *Green Thoughts* in the 1980's that gardening was a dying art, must have been surprised before her death at age 91 in 2009, that it was the number one hobby in the USA. Vegetable gardens in particular have grown by leaps and bounds, as people seek ways to eat healthier, get more exercise, and save money at the same time.

There have been many opportunities to vent my frustrations since that day back in 1986, which helps explain the rather extensive garden I created since moving to Georgia in 1993. They have run the gamut from now trivial incidents and my daughter moving over 2700 miles away, to the overwhelming anger and devastating sadness that consumed me when my oldest grandson received a mysterious brain injury at age four, as well as some serious illnesses and losses of friends and relatives. I have found acceptance and solace in my garden, which is also a good place to pray.

I even dug out most of my largest goldfish pond while listening to a radio broadcast of Ed's basketball team in a GSC tournament game one March afternoon. Anything that could go wrong did go wrong that day. The further behind we got, the harder I dug. We lost the game but I was amazed at all the work I accomplished.

I must go. The weeds are waiting. Plus it's time for some therapy—in my garden.

20 EVERBLOOMING THING

I gave my tropical hibiscus a drink and demanded, "Bloom, you idiot!" That plant was so frustrating I wanted to spray it with weed killer. In the four years I'd had it, not once had it failed to disappoint me. It was almost like it saw on my calendar when I'd be hosting something, and then timed its blooms not to coincide. It reminded me of an adorable, but obstinate three year old who continuously sings a cute song, but when asked to perform it for visitors, he refuses. Yesterday's four gorgeous red blooms now hung limp and wilted. Though there were several new buds, it was obvious not one would be blooming for our cookout that evening. I deadheaded what now looked like a large ordinary houseplant and came inside. *I ought to leave you outside this winter and be done with you for good.*

I've had a similar problem with the geraniums on my front porch. The week before I'm scheduled to host a meeting they'll be covered with beautiful blossoms; but the day all of my friends show up, I'm lucky if there's a single bloom left. I've found geraniums bloom better when fertilized with a tablespoon of Epsom Salts in a gallon of water about every two weeks; however, by late summer when temperatures stagnate in the high nineties, nothing seems to spur them on. Geraniums prefer waiting for cooler temperatures to resume their show.

One gardener friend of mine, who had to undergo an unexpected hysterectomy, decided to use her leftover birth control pills to fertilize her annuals. Instead of refusing to flower as one might expect, they bloomed profusely all summer and never looked better. A request for these pills at my age however, would only get me a referral to see a psychiatrist.

I love hydrangeas but they aren't a sure thing either, since untimely pruning or a late spring freeze can rob them of that year's blooms.

Which segues me to the subject of drying flowers in order to enjoy blooms longer. So far I've only dried hydrangea blooms using various methods with mixed results. As with so many other aspects of gardening, timing is crucial. It seems the cheap and easy methods will only work once the petals have slightly faded and changed hues. I've had success putting bunches stripped of leaves in the trunk of my car undisturbed for five sweltering hot days in mid-July. I've also dried a bloom by completely covering it with fresh cat litter in a large glass bowl and microwaving it on high for two minutes. A friend hangs them upside down in a cool dry place for several weeks but that was a royal flop for me—mine were either picked too early or the humidity in my basement was too high. Though it sounds like a complete oxymoron, I recently dried some faded long-stemmed cuttings sans leaves in a vase half full of water. As it evaporated, the blooms dried too. Next time I'll add blue fabric dye to the water to enhance the color or dab some directly on the petals.

Perhaps I should dry some geranium and hibiscus blooms to add to my obstinate plants when I have guests. But since all the cheap and easy methods are only successful once the blooms fade, that won't work with either of these.

It seems the surest way to preserve floral beauties at peak color and fullness is with silica gel. Although at $16.00 for 24 ounces, enough to dry many flowers simultaneously will be expensive, it can be used over and over.

No, silica gel is not feasible. Drying flowers as a new hobby is the only way it would be worth the investment, which does not appeal to me. Besides, dried blooms used outdoors would be too fragile to withstand the elements.

I think I'll just buy some polyester blooms to stick on my hibiscus plant for special occasions. I've already resorted to using them on my front porch when the heat causes my geraniums to stop blooming. After removing the leaves, I poke the fakes here and there among the real foliage. It would take an expert to tell the difference from the street, and only politicians, trick-or-treaters and Jehovah's Witnesses ever use the front door here in the South. I did the same thing with an attractive rusty metal planter. After two staghorn ferns failed to thrive, I stuck a plastic fern in it and hung it in a tree. It tickled me to discover mid-summer that Ed had been dousing it each time he watered my hostas and azaleas.

After all, who would suspect a Master Gardener of using fakes outdoors?

21 KEEP HERBS HANDY

Like my mother, I do not consider myself a good cook. Although I've had plenty of practice cooking for my family for four decades and even grow a few herbs, I mainly have a kitchen because it came with the house.

We dine out far less than most families and must be selective. Debilitating migraine headaches caused by allergies to food additives like MSG (Monosodium Glutamate) routinely used by restaurants and in processed foods as a flavor enhancer and preservative, make home-cooked meals the viable alternative for me. This is something of a blessing in disguise, given all the portion distortion and high salt and fat in commercially-prepared cuisine these days. Even though it's healthier to eat home cooking, it's the cleaning up I dislike most.

It has forever amused if not disgusted me to see a man take all the credit for cooking a meal when all he does is place the meat his wife has seasoned on the grill and bring it to the table when it's done (or treat his family like Gods with his burnt offerings). Meanwhile, she sets the table, gets the drinks, and prepares the salad, sides, and dessert. After everyone eats, she cleans up.

One time my oven burned out in June. It was almost Thanksgiving when it dawned on me I'd need an oven to bake my pies and turkey. My old stove had two burners that still worked, which meant my family wasn't entirely doomed to meals of cold cereal, salads and lunch meat. Besides, I rarely bake in the summer. My Yankee husband never got accustomed to homemade cornbread and biscuits. Frozen skinny dinners heat fine in the microwave, and Ed owned the king of all grills.

The solution wasn't as simple as one might think. My solid surface countertop was configured for a slide-in range, but since they cost more I opted to go with a freestanding stove and spend the savings on plants. This involved removing a thin strip of countertop in back, and the original installer had gone out of business. It took awhile to find someone else to do it and a good sale with free delivery. Nothing's easy.

Given my disdain for culinary drudgery, why do I even bother growing herbs? It's simple. In my quest to make mine the garden of my dreams (at least one of every plant and two or more of most) herbs are naturally a must. Besides, Ed and I are getting older. God forbid he should die first, I might be tempted to look for a replacement if a handyman willing to help me garden could be found and trapped. Since Mama always claimed the quickest way to a man's heart is through his stomach, merely having fresh herbs might make a better first impression on some old unsuspecting widower.

I chose a sunny plot in back for my first herb garden. The fact herbs are more flavorful when kept on the dry side and fertilized sparingly deemed them the perfect choice for a lazy gardener like me. However, they do require exceptionally good drainage. After tilling the soil deeply and adding compost and sand, my plan was to merely plant them and forget them.

Even an average cook like me has been known to garnish fresh sliced tomatoes, English peas and green beans with fresh basil. Chopped dill is great on grilled salmon, while sage, rosemary and thyme liven up ordinary chicken. I like to toss a little fresh parsley into lots of dishes. It didn't take many trips up and down stairs back and forth 40 yards in all kinds of weather to have me longing for a Segway scooter. It was easier to reach for those crusted cans half full of colorless crumbles, some so ancient they were missing a UPC code (most dried herbs have a shelf life of six months).

Though some long-lived rosemary, fennel, and garlic chives still grow in that satellite bed, my favorites such as flat parsley, basil, cilantro and dill are now in lightweight pots on the sunny deck outside my kitchen door. For seasonal color, I usually add a couple of annuals like pansies, petunias, marigolds or salvia.

I grow herbs like fennel and tansy strictly for their ornamental value and to attract butterflies and repel bugs. Making herbal soaps, sachets and potpourri does not appeal to me. Nor do I aspire to be a medicinal guru. But I do love to rub lemon balm between my hands, savoring its aroma each time I pass by.

Prior to the first fall frost, I chop and freeze annuals like basil, cilantro and dill in ice cube trays filled with water. Then I can drop a cube into whatever I'm cooking, or thaw it and press out the water to make a tasty herbal butter to spread on hot crusty bakery bread.

It's not unusual for caterpillars to strip an herb like parsley or basil of all its foliage in merely a day or two. Since pesticides are taboo around herbs, I basically try to overlook these voracious critters, ever mindful they'll soon morph into delightful butterflies that flit around and beautify my garden.

I'm always looking for ways to make gardening more convenient. I enjoy it more that way.

22 THRILLERS, FILLERS & SPILLERS

Dusting the dirt from my hands and jeans, I stepped back to admire my latest creation. "Now *that* will surely be a thriller," I said to myself, referring to the tall bronze fennel in the center of the giant lightweight pot on my deck. I'd heard that in order to create the most interest when deciding what to put in pots, gardeners should always use three plant forms: *Thrillers, Fillers* and *Spillers*. I was determined to get it right, since this pot was the focal point from my kitchen window.

It comforts me to keep my favorite herbs nearby in case the mood to cook gourmet should strike. For fillers around the fennel, I used flat parsley and both purple and green basil. For color I added a New Guinea impatiens and a coral geranium, plus white and purple 'Million Bells' petunias. I also added euphorbia 'Diamond Frost,' a tough plant with tiny white blooms which I'd proudly managed to overwinter in my basement. The huge pot was filling up fast.

For spillers, along the edge I tucked in some creeping Jenny (its chartreuse color and trailing habit are delightful), lemon thyme (which I love to rub between my hands and smell each time I pass by), and garlic chives (which is normally a filler, but mine keeps flopping over the side). The masterpiece was complete.

Things grew well as long as we had adequate rainfall and mild weather. I enjoyed subtle changes that occurred in the lovely combination each day. But by mid-June when temperatures soared into the high nineties, problems began popping up. The white 'Million Bells' petunia up and died in two days, as did the white 'Wave' petunia I bought to replace it (too much or too little water, hot sun or fertilizer—who knows?) The geranium ceased blooming. So did the New Guinea impatiens, which now begged for daily watering, to the detriment of herbs which must be kept on the dry side for best flavor. The basil and garlic chives, so tasty on fresh tomatoes from Ed's garden, bolted before they ripened. Our beagle puppy got bored one day and pulled the lemon thyme and creeping Jenny clear out of the pot, leaving them to wither and die on the deck.

The bronze fennel surprised me most. Now over six feet tall and sporting yellow blooms, it was best described as a thriller-diller bent on reaching the sky. But not to worry. Soon both the fennel and parsley were attacked by an army of large green caterpillars with black stripes. Before a hungry bird put a dent in their numbers, they devoured every trace of foliage on both plants. Knowing that with any luck the caterpillars would morph into swallowtail butterflies, I let nature take its course and did nothing. Once they disappeared to make cocoons, it looked like three green fishing rods had been poked in my once prized but now pathetic pot.

With a Fourth of July cookout on our deck fast approaching, I had to get creative. I taped three small American flags to the bare fennel stalks and filled in sparse areas with red and white gerbera daisies, with blue raffia ribbons trailing over the sides. Then I added three tall white tapered candles. Once again my container was a sight to behold. Who says only plants can be used as thrillers, fillers and spillers in pots?

When the big day arrived, we feasted on barbeque spareribs, corn on the cob, baked beans, Oriental coleslaw and watermelon. Our dessert was butter cake topped with whipped topping decorated like a flag with fresh blueberries in the top left corner for stars and rows of sliced strawberries for stripes.

We visited until dark when we turned out the lights and lit the candles. In silence we watched the fireworks show and concert broadcast outside Washington's Lincoln Center on a laptop in the comfort of our screened porch under the fan. The beauty of the sights and sounds *thrilled* our senses; our hearts *filled* with pride for the privilege of being Americans; and our gratitude *spilled* over to those who fought for the freedom we enjoy today. Our friends agreed it was one of the best Independence Day celebrations ever.

23 A FUSS-FREE FERN

Despite the slim pickings remaining at my Little Tallapoosa Botanical Society's plant swap one warm spring evening, I was determined not to leave empty-handed. I'd brought a rooted cutting of my favorite lace cap hydrangea, hoping to trade for something equally as good. Given all the bare spots in my beds, I was taking almost any plant I could find.

A woman behind me spoke up when she saw me examining a small plant with feathery foliage. "I brought that…I think it's a fern…I'm not sure what kind but it does come back every year and you don't have to water it much." Since I needed a filler for a pot on my deck, I took the fern home with me.

The little fern did extremely well in a shady spot in a large pot with a dracaena spike, red and white caladiums, a dwarf variegated hosta, a tiarella, a dragon wing begonia, three colorful impatiens and trailing small-leaf variegated ivy. Throughout the summer we enjoyed looking at that combination through the double French doors in our family room.

By mid-October the pot was so full and gorgeous it was agonizing to have to disturb it. Nonetheless, I severely cut back and repotted the begonia and dug out the caladium bulbs to save in my basement over winter. I replaced the doomed impatiens with some ornamental cabbage and vibrant pansies. Though I fully expected the first hard freeze would cause the fern, dracaena spike, and hosta to die back, to my surprise only the hosta did. The dracaena spike and fern continued to look good throughout the mild winter.

The next spring I divided my fern and put some in another pot. That fall I planted some directly in the ground. The delicate foliage was a nice contrast to the hosta, daylily and lamb's ears nearby. Again, the fern stayed mostly evergreen and spread into a larger clump that I divided and moved to several other shady spots.

I potted several up for our annual Master Gardener plant sale the following spring. Since I wasn't sure what to call it, I left the labels blank, hoping another member would know exactly what fern it was.

Several of us were trying to identify it when an outspoken woman joined us. "That's not a fern," she scoffed. "It's tansy, which is an herb. Does it get yellow flowers on it that look like clusters of little buttons?"

"No, I planted it in the shade so it probably didn't get enough sunlight to bloom."

"Tansy should be planted in full sun," she said with authority.

I felt like a child who'd been scolded by a teacher, even though I was older than she was. I couldn't wait to get home and look tansy up. I should have known the plant wasn't a fern. All ferns have tiny spores on the undersides of their fronds, prefer shade and need ample water. This plant had no spores, took full sun and was as carefree to grow as a weed. Most ferns have no smell. When rubbed between the fingers, this plant had a strong camphor odor, almost as pungent as grandma's Camphophenique ointment.

I learned other common names for tansy include 'Bitter Buttons,' and 'Yellow Buttons,' due to its flat clusters of button-size yellow flowers in late summer.

Sure enough, after moving some to a pot in full sun, by late August mine had yellow flowers, too.

Though tansy was used in the past to repel insects and also to treat a variety of ailments, modern studies discourage its medicinal use due to its adverse side effects and the fact safer, better products are available. Preparations made from tansy (essential oil, fluid extract, and tea) may contain toxic amounts of thujone which can be fatal. People have died from ingesting a mere ten drops of tansy oil!

These days tansy is mainly cultivated for naturalizing in gardens. Small amounts (fresh or minced) can be harvested from leaves and flowers and used as a pepper substitute (I'm content with using regular black pepper on my food, thank you).

I use tansy strictly for its ornamental value and to repel insects. The feathery leaves are attractive. It is tolerant of both sun and shade. It can be propagated both by seeds and division. Like most herbs, it doesn't need a lot of water to thrive. Except for an occasional snip to remove straggly, brown foliage, it's a carefree plant. Although it's not invasive, it is an opportunist; soon there will be several plants to share. The look of a fern without the fuss, and the added bonus of yellow button-like flowers—what more could I ask?

24 CAN THIS DISEASE BE CURED?

One April afternoon I was standing in the driveway when Ed came home from work. I'd spent the whole day cleaning up tons of debris, preparing for my favorite time of year—time to plant. Exhausted and filthy, I was longing for a hot shower, a bite to eat and especially my bed. Ed got out of his car, looked me over and said, "You really do need help, Shelly."

I was shocked. Had this stout sofa spud finally noticed all the upkeep for this place was more than any woman my age could handle?

"No kidding," I said.

"Yeah—help for your plantaholism. Surely even you must realize it's gotten completely out of hand."

"What in the world are you talking about?"

"I mean you need to see a shrink about why you buy so many plants. The garage floor will be covered up and here you come with another carload. It happens every spring. I ran into a psychologist after I spoke at Kiwanis Club last week. He agreed—it's an addiction."

"That's ridiculous. Counseling is the last thing I need. Of course a psychologist would say that. He's trying to make a living."

I glared at the man I'd long suspected had swallowed a huge magnet that welded his behind to the sofa springs. "What I really need is some physical help. All you do is plant a few vegetables twice a year. Then I'm expected to do everything else on hell's half acre—rake the leaves, prune the shrubs, mulch, water, fertilize, pull weeds—you name it. It's all I can do to take care of the huge flower garden I created in back. I shouldn't be saddled with this whole yarden—it's not fair!"

"Bryan does mow the grass now. You know I don't have time for or any interest in yard work."

"That still doesn't excuse you. It has to be done as long as we live in this titanic."

"So hire somebody."

"I'd have to get a job to afford that. Besides, while I've been a stay-at-home mom to Bryan the past 13 years, computers have passed me by. I'd have to go back to school for computer training before anyone would consider me for an accounting job. I do well to tend my flowers, keep this big house, do the laundry, shop, cook, handle the bills and taxes, chauffeur Bryan everywhere, plus some volunteer work on the side. Don't forget, I saved a ton of money the past two years painting this house inside and making all the drapes. I also worked full-time for over 20 years, raised three children and took care of your sick old father and spinster aunt until they died. I'm worn out."

"Use some of that money you spend on plants every year," he said.

Next morning I awoke before dawn. My aching bones creaked as I got out of bed and tiptoed downstairs to the kitchen. I hurt all over. Despite my pain, spring was my favorite season—time to get out and plant. The mere thought of what luscious delights I might find made my heart go pitter-patter. Each April, I'd go to every nursery in town to find the best deal, and then return a second time to do my buying. I chuckled. *Like an old nag finds its way back to the barn, no doubt my car could go from nursery to nursery without any steering help from me.*

I sat in my rocker, pondering Ed's accusations the night before. The mere thought of all the perennials still in pots under the deck made me admit he might be right. *Maybe I do need mental counseling.*

Ed joined me in the family room and we sipped our steaming coffee in silence. After several minutes I said, "Since...maybe I do buy too many plants—"

"Ya' think?"

"This year I'm going to dig all the holes before I ever go shopping and only buy that amount. I won't even consider buying more 'til those are in the ground."

"Good idea. Just like in AA, first you have to admit you are a plantaholic. Then put yourself on a strict budget. Take just enough cash to buy what's on your list. That'll be a step in the right direction."

"Are you crazy? I haven't used cash in years. I'll have to stop by the bank each time without a clue how much to get. What difference does it make? I pay off the credit card every month and never pay interest."

"Try it. It's a minor inconvenience when the result will be the cure. Besides, it's been proven folks buy less when paying with cash. Spend X-amount on plants and not a penny more. Do like my friend did to keep his gambling under control. He'd take $50.00 to the horse races and when it was gone, win or lose, he went home."

Before my first shopping spree I dug 360 small holes for impatiens around my ponds and river birch, torenia in two shady areas, and marigolds and vinca in my sunny terraced beds. I'd worry about pots and the front yard later.

I got $200.00 cash at the bank for ten flats of six-packs. That day I planned to see what else was available.

My first stop, right out front was a unique rusty metal arbor. It not only was to die for, but ideal for that root-bound evergreen clematis under my deck the past three years. The bad news was it cost $200.00. The good news was it wasn't a plant! Luckily, I'd stuck a credit card in my purse in case of an emergency. I panicked when I saw another woman eyeing it, since there was only one. *If that's not an emergency, what is? Besides, my birthday and Mother's Day are coming up next month. Ed is always in a quandary about what to get me. I'll be doing him a favor—he'll be so relieved.*

I paid cash for ten flats of annuals, charged the arbor, and told them I'd pick it up later.

After unloading my annuals inside the garage, I took Ed's pick-up to check out a nursery across town. Those red-tips on the north side of the house that succumbed to a virus needed replacing.

Right inside the greenhouse was a lovely espaliered coral camellia that was superb for that spot. With tax, it was over $60.00 and my cash was running low. *Instead of a new dress for the June banquet, I'll wear something old and spend that amount on plants.*

On the way to the cashier, I picked up seven 'Firepower' nandinas to replace those 'Simplicity' roses that never were; nine irresistible 'Dragon Wing' begonias for three large pots by the steps; a Carolina jessamine to replace one that died; and three lavender lantanas—the total was almost $120.00. I paid with my credit card and hurried home to unload everything before heading across town to get my arbor.

While waiting for a stop light, I spotted some gorgeous baskets of red geraniums hanging outside a store that were perfect for my front porch and deck. Last year I waited too long and they sold out. I pulled in and picked out four at $12.95 each. *Yikes! I never dreamed that new banquet dress would be so expensive.*

My fertilizer and potting soil were running low, my gloves were worn out, my best pruners were missing and one hose had sprung a leak. I also couldn't resist the last lightweight pot on sale. Surely it was all right to charge necessities as long as they weren't plants.

I was headed for the check-out line when I remembered I'd misplaced my favorite garden tool, a sturdy bricklayer's hammer. Its backside not only was great for digging planting holes and trenches for edging, but ideal for threatening Ed whenever he got obstinate. I pushed my cart aside and hurried to the tool section and found another one.

Back in line, I spotted a lone hammock. Our old rotten one was unsafe. My garden club was coming in June and two members were lawyers, possibly prone to sue. Relatives from out West were coming later that month, so everything needed to be perfect. I charged the pick-up load full of stuff and headed home for a quick drop-off before going to get my arbor.

To my dismay, when I pulled into our driveway, Ed was standing in our garage scrutinizing my purchases. I braced myself for the worst.

He eyed the arbor and glared at me. "Exactly how much cash did you take with you today, Dear?"

I gave him a sheepish look. "Not nearly enough."

"And what do you have to say for yourself?"

"Thank God...for credit cards and understanding husbands?"

He faked a smile, wrapped his arms around me, and muttered: "If you buy another plant before these are in the ground, I may leave you."

Darn! I'm going to miss you, Darlin'.

25 A BIT OF WHIMSY

Three women followed me down the slope where several stepping stones had worked loose. They hadn't been the same since Bryan rode his bicycle over them as a teen. I made a mental note to fix them.

I pointed to a family made of clay pots. "When that pottery place in Douglasville had their 25-cent sale I went a little crazy. Here are the Potters—Penelope, her kids Peter and Priscilla, and pets Puddy and Poochie. She's a single mom. Her husband left her for an empty pothead because she constantly complained about her bad hair days. But who could blame her? Look how splotchy and stringy it is." They chuckled at the three strands of straggly variegated ivy trailing from her head.

"Notice her cleavage—that Dolly Parton pot cost me eight bucks." They giggled.

"Fortunately, neither of the kids inherited their mom's hair from hell. Peter took after his father but thanks to a hungry deer, now sports a punk haircut." His liriope hair was sheared off flat and stood straight up. "Priscilla has naturally curly hair like her paternal grandmother that tends to get dry and frizzy." Asparagus fern with crispy edges trailed from her head.

"I gave up on hair for Puddy and Poochie. After several plants and even weeds failed to thrive, I bought plastic ones. When they disappeared, I used dried moss."

"Did you have instructions?" Joan asked.

"No. A magazine had a picture of a guy and his dog, but not a cat. I just used different sizes of clay pots, rebar, copper tubing, coat hangers, construction adhesive and sphagnum moss and this is the result. Birds steal the moss to make nests so it has to be replaced each year."

The Potters: Peter, Penelope (holding Priscilla),
Puddy and Poochie

I pointed to a mossy path with five Big Foot stepping stones leading into the woods. "Bryan used to have a fort at the end of that path. Spartacus, an ominous Halloween spider, lived in a giant nylon web strung between two spindly trees on the right. Bryan delighted in folks' reactions when they came up on it. But after an older woman was startled by it and almost fell, I didn't replace it after it disintegrated."

"Down Big Foot's path on your left is a natural phenomenon–a nursery log. Years ago a tulip poplar was felled by a storm but wasn't totally uprooted. Five branches on the top side grew into trees, all supported by roots on that one end. Who knows how long it will live like that. At least it's away from the house if it topples."

As we passed a hammock between sturdy posts Joan asked me, "How often do you lie down in that?"

"The next time I do will be the second time."

The women giggled. "We knew you stayed too busy taking care of this place for that," Linda said.

Barbara pointed to the paths and rock garden around the ponds. "Who did all this rock work?"

"Yours truly."

"You're kidding—by yourself?"

"Most of these rocks weigh less than the kids and grandkids we're forever lifting.

"Surely you didn't do these concrete steps."

"Yep. It stretched my strength and determination to the limit and was so physically hard, it made me cry. But somehow I got it done and vowed never to mix concrete in a wheelbarrow again."

"I'd say you're a glutton for punishment."

"I'd really rather not do any heavy physical labor around my house and garden. But I'm so impatient and persnickety it's easier to do it myself than try to delegate or go to the bother and expense of hiring help. Ed claims he enjoys the act of gardening whereas I'm results-oriented—the end justifies the means. Aside from the satisfaction and relief a job is finished, I don't find the work itself very gratifying."

"So you did all this without any help from Ed?"

"Ed and Bryan helped get rocks at a construction site and also my son-in-law, Matt, when he visited us. They unloaded them at the top of the slope, and then I rolled them down hill and built the falls and rock garden. Our oldest son, who is 6' 10" tall and a former college athlete who plays golf and works out regularly, has never liked doing manual labor. The first time Sean brought his fiancée to visit us, I was shocked when he volunteered to help Ed unload rocks as Kristen watched in awe of his brute strength. But after they were married, Sean never touched another rock!"

"We bought four pallets of field stones and I made the paths. Ed shoveled crushed gravel out of his pick-up for the base. But his demanding job left him little time to help me situate stones and build steps."

We passed by a statue holding a jug. "Most Rebeccas at the Well are topless," I said. "With so many of Bryan's 12-year-old friends around, I paid dearly to get one fully clothed." They laughed.

I pointed to a group of wooden birdhouses on poles that Bryan and I painted when he was 13. "This is Birdville, USA. Population: who knows, or cares? Step around back to see Bryan's big python crawling up the backside of Grouse House Hotel." There were two signs on the three-story birdhouse: "Rooms" and "Cheep-cheep." "To the left is the Albatross Academy where fledglings take singing and flying lessons," I said.

"Too cute," Joan said.

"The white gazebo is the Front Perch Restaurant. The church is the Love Dove Chapel. Dr. Quack is on the end—notice the Rx symbol advertising various seeds, worms and insects to cure bird ailments. The Carroll County Ag Center has a Georgia Master Gardener license plate for its roof. The red one with two chimneys is Plume Preeners, the local beauty shop. The blue barn with the owl in its loft is Owl's Feed & Seed."

"I think I'll paint some birdhouses for my garden," Barbara said.

"It was fun. It's hard to find things a teenager and his mom can do together."

"You got that right," said Linda, the mother of three grown sons.

I pointed to an NCAA Final Four basketball on a stand flanked by Sean's size 16 sneakers planted with zinnias. "That's our coach's gazing ball. Every basketball coach dreams of going to the NCAA Final Four Tournament. Ed's team made it 1970, when he was assistant to Coach Lou Henson at NMSU. Ed's UWG team made it to the Division II Elite Eight Tournament in 2002."

"I'm impressed," they said in unison.

We walked toward a circular bed of Knockout roses. "Where did you get that statue from the Garden of Good and Evil?" Barbara asked.

"It was a birthday gift from Sean and Kristen. She's a replica of Savannah's famous bird girl. I bought the tall concrete stand so she'd be above the roses."

We passed by a copper sundial engraved "Grow old along with me; the best is yet to be."

"I bet that was an anniversary present from Ed," Barbara said.

"To each other—but I picked it out. The amazing thing is that we haven't killed each other...yet! At times I thought this garden would be the death of us. It helps that we each have our own turf. Ed grows edibles while I do ornamentals."

"I can only imagine how much work it was."

"And still is. I don't have as much yard art as some do. Too much can detract from the plants. The important thing about a garden is that it reflects your personality and contains what you like. Of course yard art changes over time—wood rots; iron rusts; paint chips and fades. Ed proved concrete isn't permanent when he backed over my Chihuahua and broke its nose and ears."

"Now that Ed's retired, downsizing has appeal. The upkeep on this place gets harder every year. But I dread the day we have to leave it, for whatever reason. We've got too much invested in it, not only money, but blood, sweat and tears. Our roots run deep, both literally and figuratively. I'd love to keep it in the family, or leave it to one of our kids. But our oldest two are settled on opposite sides of the country. Maybe if Bryan finds a job in this area after college, he'll want it. The past few years, whenever we've asked him to help us clean the ponds or do other garden chores, Bryan claims he hates it. He was only four when we moved here. This garden and woods down to the creek were such an integral part of his life he called them 'Bryan's World.' Deep down, I suspect he loves this place as much as we do."

Despite the fact this garden demands as much work as it gives pleasure, it's my sanctuary and a part of me. I want it left intact to be cared for and enjoyed by future generations of my family. My fear is that strangers will buy it and decide it requires too much upkeep and expense. They'll level it to the ground and plant loblolly pines like those the tornado felled in 1992.

A lump formed in my throat and my voice cracked. "Only time will tell." I said, turning aside as a tear ran down my cheek.

26 KEEPING UP WITH THE JONESES

Thank goodness in my neighborhood there's no pressure to keep up with the Joneses. No, in my subdivision it's the Smiths—namely one W.H. Smith. Not only does this man have years of gardening experience, he's even served as President of the Georgia Master Gardener Association. Talk about pressure!

Now I've noticed being a certified Master Gardener doesn't necessarily mean you'll have the best-looking yard on your block. Many new members get so busy doing volunteer work, they tend to let things slide at home. At least I hope folks get that impression whenever they round my cul-de-sac after passing by W.H.'s Garden of Eden.

From the street, it looks like the Master Gardener living at my house has died. I'm currently blaming it on the awful drought we've had for several years. The Bermuda grass sod the original landscaper installed two decades ago succumbed to both neglect and shade of maturing trees. Mother Nature graciously replaced that grass with native moss, bare spots and weeds.

All the good stuff in our yard is planted behind our house which may explain why we've only been on our city's "hidden" garden tour. In retrospect, the selection committee must have been desperate. Or perhaps they had a last-minute cancellation.

We have plenty of excuses for our pathetic front yard. Before Ed retired, he had a full-time demanding job and a large vegetable garden as his hobby. But he's also the reason I declined the offer of a free Irish Setter once by saying, "No thanks—I married one and have three pups." I've been a stay-at-home mom for over 20 years to our youngest son who is now in college. Though I aspired for years to be Martha Stewart, lacking her limitless budget and full-time staff caused me to fall way short of my goal. I'm also an avid reader and aspiring writer, which take way too much of my time. So in the spring and fall when garden duties frequently consume entire days, I do well to keep my family clean, fed and a path cleared up the stairs to my bed, ready for my nightly collapse. There are numerous plants in pots under my deck that have been begging for several years to be planted. We've kept enough indoor pets through the years to justify hiring a full-time zookeeper. Our basement looks like the set of a horror movie. The list of things I want to accomplish would overflow a tall file cabinet. You get the picture.

In sharp contrast, W.H. and his wife, Peggy have it all so together in every respect—impeccably groomed, nary a hair out of place. He always puts down plastic in his trunk when hauling plants and removes his shoes before going inside. Everything's all neat and perfect throughout the Smiths' lovely home and yard. Both now retired, Peggy sees to the household and W.H. does all the yard work. They host nice parties with scrumptious food. They're active in their church and other social and volunteer activities. They travel abroad and also manage to spend quality time with their two young grandchildren in Atlanta.

One day about six years ago I passed by W.H.'s house, which is always necessary to get to and from my home. Right in front was yet another garden club's "Yard of the Month" sign. It's practically a semi-annual event. He has the most beautiful flowerbed running the length of his front yard right out by the street, with a yard full of assorted shade-loving beauties for a backdrop that's unbelievable. The place always looks like a scene from the cover of *Southern Living* magazine. By mixing a variety of evergreens, annuals and perennials with differing bloom times, he has continuous color in every season just like all the experts recommend. If I'm ever involved in a head-on collision, it will surely be in front of his house because I am so distracted. Each time I pass by his beautiful yard it makes my day.

I was tired of working like a slave and only being a qualifier for "Weed of the Week." That day a bolt from the blue struck me. Although my pie-shaped lot was too narrow at the street for planting much, there was space for a nice flower border in front of the trees along my long sloping curved driveway. With its morning sun and afternoon shade, the site seemed perfect for a host of plants that could be enjoyed by passersby each time they rounded the cul-de-sac.

Intent on making this the best border in my yard and possibly the entire subdivision, that fall I enlisted Ed's help hauling in topsoil and amendments. I even had a separate soil test done. After searching through magazines and catalogs, I carefully selected the best plants. Azaleas, spring bulbs, iris, daylilies, re-blooming hydrangeas, mums and asters, plus spots reserved for seasonal annuals, would ensure a succession of blooms throughout the year. I also placed a pricey decorative white birdhouse feeder with a copper roof at the far end of my driveway for a focal point.

After everything was planted, fertilized, and mulched, I watered my new bed religiously. It was certain to be the envy of the entire neighborhood, perhaps even W.H. Smith. I couldn't wait.

To my dismay, my prized bed was a gross disappointment. What I failed to consider was that Bryan and his friends would soon be learning to drive. Before I knew it, half a dozen testosterone-riddled adolescents were practicing rapid reverse maneuvers on my long crooked driveway, usually in the dark. During the next year, except for three azaleas safely nestled among trees, the teenagers not only managed to run over every single plant in that bed; they even backed over my mailbox, too!

W.H. never even suspected what a threat I almost was. Oh well...now that area along the driveway matches the rest of our pathetic front yard again.

27 THE BUCK STOPS HERE

Ed had just gone back to work after lunch when I looked out my kitchen window and saw something large, tan and strange among his vegetables. When the objects moved, it dawned on me that deer—six in all—were feasting on Ed's green tomatoes.

Our fat lazy beagle was in the family room snoozing on the sofa under the fan. I yelled the only command Clementine ever obeyed: "Quick, come get a treat!" She opened her eyes, stretched her limbs, and took her time getting down off the sofa. With treat in hand, I coaxed her out the back door onto the deck.

I clapped my hands and yelled at the deer, "Get out of here you varmints!" Clementine perked up her ears and managed a "woof." The deer raised their heads and stared as I ran down the stairs screaming and flailing my arms as if bees were inside my bra. Clementine was right behind me, anxious to get her treat.

When the deer saw we were coming toward them, they turned and calmly walked the other way. Clementine stopped this side of Ed's garden and uttered several "woof-woofs" as she watched the deer disappear in single file into the woods.

I gave her the treat. "Sorry worthless dog," I said, knowing she likely couldn't help the fact her nose was defective for her breed. It was my fault, for insisting Ed replace Ruff with an unregistered female beagle in hopes she'd be part mutt and have characteristics the neighbors and I wouldn't find so obnoxious.

As long as our first beagle was alive, we never had any deer problems, nor did any of our neighbors. Ruff would have chased these intruders until they all collapsed in utter exhaustion. I learned the hard way that all beagles are not created equal. When a Georgia redneck claims a breeder has the best beagles, he means the best huntin' dogs. Take caution from the voice of experience: huntin' beagles are not the best pets for a subdivision. They can quickly alienate the neighbors.

Folks are forever asking me, "How can I stop deer from devouring my plants?" As urban sprawl has overtaken their habitats, they are no longer hunted regularly to control their numbers, which are said to be higher here now than when the Pilgrims landed. Deer easily adapt to a diet of vegetables and ornamentals they scavenge from yards and gardens. They are also a traffic menace, and spread Lyme's Disease to us through ticks.

It seems the only certainty with deer is that nothing is certain. Just as humans do, deer prefer some plants over others. Favorite plants in one area may be left untouched in another. Yet a starving deer will eat almost anything, which is why plants may be labeled "deer resistant" but not "deer proof."

Deer favorites in my garden include flowering quince, Indian Hawthorne, golden euonymous, hosta, roses, passion flower, azaleas, pansies and impatiens. Trees they've munched on include cherry, dogwood, and redbud. Some say they like daylilies and clematis, but they have not eaten mine so far. To date, they have shown no interest in my other perennials.

As for garden edibles, deer like most things humans do except for onions, garlic, rosemary, thyme, asparagus, summer squash, hot peppers and potatoes. They love our peas, green beans, cucumbers, corn, tomatoes, watermelon, cantaloupe and small berries.

After deer continuously feasted on three golden euonymus shrubs, I decided to get rid of them. My friend

Eleanor advised me to keep a few favorites around the edges as sacrifice plants, or else they would start eating my other ornamentals. Sometimes onions or lantana planted around the perimeter will turn them away. But if these four-legged foragers are hungry enough, they will leap over these to get to their favorites.

When my prized weeping cherry sustained severe damage to its trunk on two sides about two feet from the ground one winter, I expected to lose it. Apparently a buck either tried to sharpen his antlers on it, or tore off and ate strips of bark. Thankfully, it only happened once and the tree is gradually healing itself.

Like other gardeners through the ages, we have tried various methods to keep deer at bay. Since deer seem leery of the color white, we've surrounded vegetables with white rope and tied white plastic garbage bags on poles to flap in the wind. We've strung old CD discs and aluminum pie tins on strings to flash white in the dark and scare them away. Ed has spread both human and dog hair around in hopes it will send deer packing. He's also hung pieces of strong-smelling soap in the toes of white socks on poles among his vegetables. Since human urine is said to be an effective deterrent, he regularly applies it around the perimeter of his garden. We're too technically challenged to rig up motion detectors like some do that cause lights to come on or a spray of water to scare them away. A woman in the country protects her 250 tea roses by scattering old blaring radios among them. Sometimes a method will work for awhile and then something new must be tried.

Two years ago Ed solved his problem by installing an eight-foot nylon mesh fence around his vegetable plot. However, this fence will not keep out rabbits, which are not a problem since we have pets.

Now that Ed's garden is fenced, I must keep an eye out for deer in mine. At the first sign of damage, I spray their favorites with a commercial concentrate made from garlic and rotten eggs that cannot be used on vegetables. Fortunately, the odor dissipates shortly. It must also be reapplied after a rain, but it is effective.

Neighbors in the center of our subdivision over seed their Bermuda lawn with rye grass every winter to assure a green lawn year round. Deer find it irresistible, so they go through other yards to reach it, including ours, and snack on favorite ornamentals along the way.

Smaller varmints can also be a problem. W.H. Smith has resorted to planting prized hostas in pots due to voles or chipmunks which eat the roots (at least this is the excuse he gave Peggy for purchasing a colorful assortment of pricey ceramic beauties). The fact our outdoor cats, Doom and Ivan, are good hunters and our current beagle, Elvira, loves to chase critters helps prevent damage in our gardens. As long as we only fed the cats dry food, they regularly hunted voles, squirrels, chipmunks and rabbits. Sadly, they also killed birds. Now that Ed spoils them daily with canned cat food, they are not such avid hunters. Last summer the sated cats let voles gnaw roots off five nandina 'Firepower.' Prior to planting replacements, I loosely wrapped the root balls in leftover pet screen from our porch.

Friends claim armadillos are among the worst culprits the way they dig and ravage an area to reach grubs and worms. As yet, none have come here and I hope they won't, although Bryan has seen them at the creek. Again, our pets may be a deterrent.

A friend's native country garden got ravaged by a wild hog the day he hosted our garden club. It was astounding a single animal could do so much damage; like a bulldozer driven by a drunk had come through.

*Garden Guardians hard at work: Elvira, Doom, and
Ivan the Terrible (who's actually not so bad).*

Snakes can also pose a serious threat. Rat and king snakes have dropped in through the years, but the poisonous copperhead Ed killed under our deck put the fear in us. Two weeks later he almost stepped on a baby copperhead in our garage that got away. Now we fear that snake and its siblings are lurking in our yard, making us squeamish to be working out there.

There will always be wildlife here because of woods and a creek behind our property. I've considered having my garden certified as a wildlife habitat but never have. I normally try to live with and ignore wildlife until it becomes a serious nuisance.

28 SACRIFICE SOLUTION

"What has that crazy woman done now?" Ed grumbled as he trudged across the deck and came inside. I'd been dreading this moment for the past three days.

He glared at me and said, "I cannot believe you cut down my favorite tree while I was at my meeting last week. You know I loved those two Japanese maples growing side by side, especially in fall when the Bloodgood turned bright red and the green one changed to orange. For God's sake, why did you do it? Have you overdosed on insecticide fumes?"

"I can't tell you how much I hated to do it. But it was a...Sophie's—uh Shelly's choice....due to a Siamese twin situation."

He wrinkled his brow. "A what?"

"It's like twin babies joined at the hip who share vital organs. Sometimes if you insist on leaving them like Chang and Eng you'll lose them both. First you agonize; then you decide which one has the best chance of survival; and ultimately, sacrifice the other one. Heinous as it is, that's all you can do."

"Those two maples weren't joined at the hip! They were at least four feet apart!"

"With canopies 20 feet wide at maturity. They grew more distorted by the day with that dogwood towering over them. They needed more sun to thrive."

"I loved the way the green one hovered over the Bloodgood—almost like a protector."

"Protector my foot! More like a thief, the way it stole all the sunlight, causing them both to grow lopsided. Besides, it was embarrassing to me as a Master Gardener. Years ago when I bought those twiggy blue light specials,

I was clueless they'd get so large. I realized later they were planted too close together and in too much shade."

"That's ridiculous. Thousands of trees in the woods grow close together."

"Yeah, straight up like telephone poles. I pointed out to you before you left that several limbs on the Bloodgood were shriveling up and dying. It hadn't recuperated from our big Easter freeze when the worst drought in Georgia's history struck. Do you realize the total outdoor watering ban has been on now for almost a month? After you left, I noticed half the Bloodgood's limbs had shriveled leaves, and the green maple had major branches dying. It was obvious their roots were in a battle for both water and nutrients. The soil in that area is also crummy and full of rocks. I had to act fast. The pond and waterfall liners kept the Bloodgood from getting water and nutrients on one side and with the other maple too close, they were both about to croak."

He frowned. "You couldn't possibly have waited until I got back to see what I thought?"

"No, I couldn't. This garden is my domain and I'm the chief tree surgeon here. So with God's help, I'll make the life and death decisions. You're forever telling me to do whatever I want in my flower garden and you'll do as you please in your vegetable patch. Besides, you never would have agreed to sacrifice one. You'd have done nothing and lost them both. We may lose the Bloodgood, anyway, if it doesn't rain soon. It just breaks my heart to see my garden in such decline. June's always peak time and it's never looked worse."

He sighed. "My garden isn't going to make anything this year either, hot as it is with no rain."

"At least it's still legal to water vegetables. I guess you noticed my impatiens and ferns completely croaked.

Now even the daylilies are turning yellow and dying. Yesterday I cut my roses and shrubs back by a third so they can make do with less water. The news says they're fining cheaters in Atlanta for watering outdoors now. They'll be doing that here before long."

"Yeah, it's pathetic," he said, shaking his head.

My voice cracked as my eyes flooded with tears. "Surely you don't think I wanted to chop down a Japanese maple. I bawled the whole time. All week I've made Bryan put in the stopper during his 20-minute showers. It takes him seven trips to haul his bath water down the stairs in buckets and dump it on the two in front. Bob and Andy planted the Bloodgood in 2000 in memory of Mama. I just can't lose it, if I can help it."

He wrapped his arms around me as I broke down sobbing. "It's tough. Hang in there, Babe. Something's got to give soon. Your cousins in the Southwest are drowning this year."

"I know. I guess floods are worse. There is one bright spot on the horizon, though."

"What—is Bryan finally taking shorter showers?"

"As a matter of fact, he is. But I found a tiny seedling under the green Japanese maple and put it in a pot before I sawed the mother tree down. I'll keep it on the deck until it's larger; then I'll set it out in a special spot as a memorial to the 2007 drought."

He smiled, and gave me a kiss.

29 WEED OR PRIZED PERENNIAL

While working in the shrub section at our annual Master Gardener plant sale I overheard a customer say, "This is the last thing I expected to find here today. Can you believe Master Gardeners are selling weeds?"

We had tried our best to cull out undesirables ahead of time, like the healthy tray of poison ivy an intern unknowingly donated. When I turned around I was startled to see the offending plant was leatherleaf mahonia, a favorite of mine. I was certain it was listed in a book at home as one of the 400 best garden plants.

I couldn't resist asking her, "Do you have this shrub in your yard?"

The brunette shook her head. "No, but you see it growing everywhere. I'm sure it's native to Georgia, which means it's a weed."

"Actually, it's not native here, but it does reseed easily," I said. "It's called Japanese mahonia or Oregon grape in other areas, but it originated in China."

Her blond friend wrinkled her nose. "The last thing I need is something that reseeds all over my yard."

"As weeds go, they're easy to pull. Plus it's a slow grower, so it'll be several years before that happens." I asked the brunette, "Do you like to attract birds and butterflies to your yard?"

"Yes. That's why I'm here today."

"Then if you have shade or at least an afternoon shady spot in your yard, you'll want one of these. It even loves our acid red clay soil. Being evergreen, the handsome foliage looks good year-round. It also gets pretty yellow blossoms shaped like fingers that will perfume your whole garden in mid-winter."

Amused by their aroused interest in the plant, I kept on. "In spring birds love to eat the luscious blue berries that form like clusters of grapes every winter. Their gnarly stalks and stiff prickly leaves give them visual interest, especially when light dapples on them through trees. Plus this is *the* shrub for those who hate to prune since it looks best when left to grow naturally. I loved the one I had in Mississippi so much it was the first plant I bought when I moved here."

I couldn't resist. "Plant one in front of a window and you won't have to worry about burglars. Those sharp prickly spines on leaf tips will send them somewhere else looking for their next victim."

The blond spoke up. "I could plant a hedge row by my driveway to keep those obnoxious neighbor kids from cutting through my yard."

The duo was salivating when I added, "I love to use cuttings for Christmas decorations. They look like giant holly. I've even sprayed them gold and silver. The leaf bracts look so pretty with pine greenery on wreaths and swags for the front door, window sills and mailbox. Add a cheerful red bow, some pinecones, glass balls or fake fruit. Voila! You're ready for Christmas."

It tickled me when the women loaded all nine remaining pots onto their cart. Just further proof that given the right information, one gardener's weed might turn into her prized perennial.

(Woops! I apologize, ladies. I just learned that although leatherleaf mahonia is a minor problem in Georgia natural areas these days, it is now regarded as invasive in adjacent states. Just further proof that one gardener's favorite perennial could indeed turn out to be a weed.)

30 WICKER BICKER

I have always yearned for a garden room. The inviting ones on magazine covers leave me salivating, with their classic white wicker furniture with colorful cushions and lush green ferns. They look like the ideal spot to spend a lazy summer afternoon with a good book under a fan sipping unsweet iced tea with lemon (none of that hummingbird juice for me). The main reason I've always wanted a garden room, however, is for keeping tender plants over the winter.

When we inherited some antique wicker in 1988, my desire for a garden room grew more acute. But with children to educate, it wasn't in the budget. I put various pieces in our bedrooms and covered the cushions to match each room's décor. It's good the set had no sofa, because we already had wall-to-wall furniture.

When the 18-year-old wooden deck at our current house declined to the point of being scary, especially after learning it didn't comply with current safety codes, we had to act. We made an appointment with an Atlanta company that built garden rooms to give us an estimate.

The dapper slick-talking salesman arrived late with the excuse that when he'd stopped along the way to give another woman an estimate, her deck collapsed with both of them on it. When he added, "Luckily her deck wasn't high off the ground like yours and neither of us got hurt," we were skeptical. Though his verbal quote was higher than we hoped, he insisted we come to their Atlanta showroom to see the high quality of their materials before making a decision.

Following a demonstration of various features, we sat in a sample garden room while they worked up a price.

Then they insulted our intelligence by doubling the salesman's initial quote and applying various discounts. The end result was a higher quote for a smaller room. After learning that price did not include demolition and hauling away of our old deck as initially promised, and that sunrooms also require heating and cooling, which was extra, we nixed it in the bud.

Next, I called several local companies for estimates on replacing our deck and adding a screened porch. Though disappointed, I knew a porch was more practical and could be used in three seasons in Georgia's mild climate. At last I'd have a place for my wicker.

When I insisted on using the latest composite decking and sturdy pet screen, Ed quipped, "Why is it when folks get old as dirt, they want things that will last?" One contractor seemed to bite his tongue to keep from telling us regular pressure-treated wood would suffice at our age.

Since two contractors never got back to us with quotes and two others were not licensed and insured, we went with the fifth one's estimate.

The project progressed smoothly and I was relieved there was minimal damage to my plants. The new porch not only turned out nicer than we dreamed, but at last we had the perfect spot for viewing the garden while sitting in our antique wicker. I couldn't wait.

Next morning I moved all the wicker pieces to the new porch and reserved a spot for the wicker sofa in our garage that my friend Carol sold me after Ed insisted on having one for taking naps. A fresh coat of white paint and new cushion covers I planned to make would have everything looking terrific. I was pleased.

On Ed's lunch break I watched from the kitchen window as he wriggled his big rear into the rocker. He reminded me of Papa Bear in Goldilocks' chair. When he suggested we eat out there, I carried him his plate.

I had just turned around to go get mine when I heard a c-r-a-c-k! Pop! Bam! When Ed perched on the end of the wicker chaise, it collapsed, scattering his lunch around the floor. I wanted to cry. After waiting 20 years for a place for my wicker, it wasn't going to work.

"Throw out this antique junk and get something we can sit on out here!" Ed demanded, as Bryan helped me pull him up from the floor. "I never liked this stuff as a child when Aunt Marg had it on her porch in Syracuse. Back then it was Pepto-Bismol pink!"

"All right," I said. "But it's going to cost you."

"Whatever it takes," he grumbled.

After finding nothing local, I bought a Nassau seven-piece deep seating set with cushions and matching dinette in black powder coated aluminum on the internet. Though pricey, shipping was free. Two weeks later when it was delivered, we learned it also had to be assembled, which took us the better part of two days.

I made a tablecloth and eight throw pillows from indoor-outdoor fabric. The space was further enhanced with houseplants, hanging planters, wall art, a rug and candelabra for the table. It looked terrific.

Carol was glad to buy back her sofa. Seems she regretted selling it after her front porch looked so bare. The other wicker was relegated to the basement awaiting a fresh coat of paint and new cushions. Since Bryan was moving to his own apartment, I decided to redo his old bedroom and use it in there for guests.

The enjoyment this outdoor room has brought us has us regretting we didn't add it years ago...now if only I had a good spot to overwinter tender plants.

31 JUST SAY "NO"

Nothing starts a gardener's adrenalin rushing faster than having to shape her place up for a tour. The days rush by like scenery from a train that's speeding past a station, making her wonder how she'll ever get it ready in time. When the visitors are one's very own Master Gardener group, the pressure intensifies.

Sweat rolled down my face as I ripped open a huge box delivered three weeks later than expected. Inside was a deluxe Nantucket arbor, a birthday present I'd bought myself from Ed. Here it was Friday already, only six days until they were coming.

I was running more behind than usual. Redoing the beds around our new deck, building a new brick landing by the stairs, and installing a new flower bed out front took longer than I anticipated. These chores were in addition to those of a typical spring—raking up debris, planting, weeding, mulching and cleaning ponds.

Per the enclosed instructions, I unpacked and checked off each part. When I realized one thin 12-inch slat was missing, I panicked. There was no way that piece could be added later. This behemoth had to be assembled in strict order.

I called the company. The man apologized and said, "We'll send another one right away. It should arrive there next Wednesday."

"Next Wednesday!" I said in horror. "A hundred Master Gardeners will be here next Thursday night."

"Oh...well we've been known to overnight a part for a special occasion, like a wedding. Let's see...you should have that piece by 3:00 p.m. tomorrow."

Though I was skeptical, I nearly fell over when the slat arrived from Canada at 10:00 next morning!

That afternoon I assembled the arch but knew the instructions didn't lie. It would take two strong men to wrestle the sides with two four-by-fours inside each one down the stairs and then connect them to the arch.

On Saturday, Ed and Bryan were skeptical as they perused all the parts and screws scattered around the garage. "You should have called Frank to do this," Ed grumbled, anxious to get back to his game on TV. Our friend had helped us with some home improvement projects the previous winter.

"I did. Frank's either out of town or he saw it was us, knew something needed fixing and didn't answer." Ed shook his head.

"We can do this, guys. It's not rocket science. Just slip the four hollow PVC posts over those eight-foot wooden ones there. After I attach them to these lattice centers y'all can carry the sides down the stairs. We'll dig four holes, level the sides, attach the arch and fill around the posts with concrete mix. It'll look so pretty."

Ed picked up a wooden four-by-four and shoved it into the wrong end of the PVC post. It went part way in and wouldn't budge. As Bryan and Ed tried to wrench it loose, they looked like conquistadors forcing battering rams into the gate of an enemy's castle.

When Ed told Bryan to get the WD-40, I cringed. Sure enough, the end they sprayed was so slippery they couldn't hold onto it. I went to the basement and got a sledge hammer and a small board. We took turns hammering the post. After 20 minutes we forced it out.

"It can't be done, Shelly," Ed said. "Those pressure-treated posts won't fit inside these hollow PVC things." He went inside to watch his ball games.

I wanted to cry. No way was I packing up all these parts to return this monstrosity. I decided to whittle the edges of the boards with a knife to see if that might do the trick.

Thank goodness it worked. Two hours later we had the sides assembled. Ed and Bryan hoisted the cumbersome things down the stairs. By the time we got the holes dug and leveled, the arch attached, and the posts set in concrete, it was suppertime. As we high-fived one another, all I could think of was the tsunami of chores yet to be done.

I could kick myself for getting suckered into this again. When will I ever learn to just say "No?" I should have known from being on a garden tour seven years before how hectic the last few days would be. It's like the mother of a toddler who decides to have another child. She forgets what an ordeal the first birth was.

One of my biggest faults is underestimating how much time a chore will take, especially when preparing for an event. As the deadline approaches, it seems time is a maniac in a monster truck right on my heels trying to run me over and do me in. Plus I'm a terrible procrastinator. If it weren't for the last minute, I'd never get anything done.

Time is our most precious resource and mine is perpetually in short supply. I'll never forget a pushy woman's reply when I told her I didn't have time to take over her charity. Prior to hanging up in a huff, she said, "You have 24 hours in a day just like the rest of us."

I always start out with a list. Crossing off a completed task gives me a sense of accomplishment. But it discourages me how often, after working the entire day, not a single chore is finished. My yarden is so large that tasks such as winter clean-up and mulching can take me up to a month or longer.

As a do-it-yourselfer with an eye for details and a bent toward perfectionism, I often fall way short of my goal. What I really am is a frustrated procrastinating perfectionist who never gets it all done the way I want it in the allotted time frame. This year was no exception.

Sunday evening I turned my attention to a rusted brown arbor made from hollow steel, another birthday gift I'd bought myself from Ed. Strong winds felled a branch which knocked the arbor into Ed's deer fence and broke a corner piece that connected the arch. With no time to have it welded, my temporary fix was to put a large gutter nail inside to support the break and fill in space around it with construction adhesive. But first I wanted to paint the arbor white so it would show up better. That night I spread out plastic tarps in the garage and applied the first coat. Between other chores next day I sprayed more. It took eight cans to cover it.

On Tuesday's lunch break, Ed was helping me carry the arch to the side yard to install it, when the exact same piece broke off the opposite corner. I wired it together and hoped no one would notice.

I planned to plant the evergreen clematis that had been in a pot under my deck for several years on the arbor but the red clay soil in that spot was petrified and unyielding. I found a large clay pot in the basement, plopped the clematis inside, covered the top with dried moss, and wound the shoots up through the sides.

On Wednesday I touched up several bird houses with fresh paint and put new moss around the pot people. Since the concrete was dry around the new arbor, I planted a 'New Dawn' rose on one side and moved a pink hybrid honeysuckle to the other. The rest of the day I frantically pulled weeds, watered impatiens and hydrangeas, and deadheaded blossoms. Though it was heart-wrenching to pinch off gorgeous daylily blooms, it saved time I wouldn't have next morning. That afternoon Bryan mowed the lawn.

After a hasty supper of leftovers, I vacuumed the screened porch and furniture, washed the tablecloth, and spot-cleaned all the outdoor cushions. Then I made new covers for the throw pillows on the hammock. It was after midnight when I collapsed into bed.

Next morning my feet hit the floor running. After a bowl of cold cereal with blueberries and coffee, I blew off the deck, garage, and driveway, raked up sunflower seed debris under Ed's bird feeders and swept off the stone paths. To avoid embarrassment, I tacked pieces of black landscape fabric over the basement windows to hide the deplorable mess there wasn't time to clean. After washing down a peanut butter sandwich with a glass of iced tea, I cleaned the house downstairs.

With time running out and so much to do, my heart was racing, making me wonder whether I'd survive this ordeal. An old quote came to mind: "Everything in this life takes longer than you think except life itself."

I chopped pecans and mixed up brownies for the Master Gardeners' potluck supper. While they baked I dragged my achy bones upstairs to shower and dress. I barely made it to the Ag Center by 6:30. The plan was for members to eat and have a business meeting before touring my garden and W.H. Smith's up the street.

Everyone had filled their plates when rain began pounding the Ag Center's tin roof, so loud we couldn't converse. I wanted to cry. As the crow flies, our subdivision was only a mile away. Now no one would probably even bother to come see our gardens. I thought of all the hours toiled in vain, and wondered if W.H. was near collapse, too.

Ten minutes later the rain stopped. I slipped out early and rushed home—it hadn't rained at my house at all. It was so calm I lit the candelabra over the table and plopped into a chair beside my ponds. Though so exhausted I was punch-drunk, my garden had never looked better.

We had a good turnout and everyone seemed to have a good time. Though I was barely hanging on by the seeds of my plants when the last guest left at 9:30, I was ecstatic the last garden tour I'd ever have in my life was over.

Some people never learn. The following May found me hosting my Little Tallapoosa Botanical Society meeting in my garden. *Are all avid gardeners hopeless exhibitionists? Or is it just me?*

32 THE RIGHT PLANT FOR THE SITE

In the process of relocating to Georgia, we looked at a number of houses for sale. Among them was a brand new white brick house in an attractive subdivision. Though the price was too high, our realtor told us the builder would take an offer.

The front lawn of hybrid Bermuda sod was nice, and I was impressed with four evergreens used as foundation plants in front that were already over six feet tall, which to me meant they were expensive.

Aside from the fact the carpet, cabinets and walls were also white, the house didn't have enough bedrooms and the dining room was too small for our rug and furniture. It was also too close to a busy street since Bryan was only four. So we didn't make an offer on it.

Several years later, I was glad we hadn't. Since the house we did buy was at the end of that same street, we drive past it each time we go somewhere. Within five years those four evergreens were over twice as tall as the house, about to overtake it. It seems they were Leyland cypress, which under ideal conditions can grow to be 100 feet tall and 50 feet wide! The owner had to have them removed before they compromised the foundation.

The house we bought had three Nellie Stephens hollies along its front foundation which grew to be small trees in only four years. Aside from being planted too close to the house, they overtook the sidewalk leading to the porch and were clearly too large for their sites. Insect infestations caused unsightly damage to the leaves and the remedy involved annual treatment with dormant spray, which can damage a home's siding. I eventually cut them down and had the stumps ground.

I realized too late the 'Heavenly Bamboo' nandinas we chose as replacements were not the best, although the shrub has its attributes. The leaves have interesting shapes; the foliage changes color with the seasons; and in winter, it has attractive clusters of red berries which I and the birds love. But they require entirely too much pruning to shape and contain their rampant growth. They also spread by underground shoots which constantly need digging out. Nandinas are now regarded by some as garden thugs, and the reason I call mine damninas.

A large crape myrtle with an exceptionally attractive trunk was also planted too close to our home's northeast corner in back by the original owner. Though the shrub bloomed profusely in midsummer in a lovely cherry, it grew so tall its branches scraped the siding and even the gutters on our second story. For awhile, every year I took my hand saw and loppers to it and performed crape murder. But after hurricane-like winds caused its branches to damage our spotlight, it had to go. It broke my heart to cut down such a prized specimen.

Another house on my street has a lovely red Japanese maple in an alcove in its front façade. Now it's beginning to outgrow this spot, which means it will eventually require disfiguring pruning or total removal.

On the way into town, for several years I watched two Leyland cypress trees next to a mobile home get enormous. Two years ago, a new house was built in the rear. Then one day the trailer disappeared, leaving the towering trees oddly situated in the new home's front yard. Oh well, a zealous homeowner with a gigantic ladder and a discount store's entire inventory of colored lights could land them in the *Guinness Book of World Records* as the tallest twin Christmas trees.

The large island in another yard has numerous shrubs and trees planted so close together they seem to shout at me, "Too much is never enough!" They've grown into a massive weedy conglomeration that obscures half the house from the street. I'd like to assume a kung-fu posture and whack everything to the ground, in hopes only a few will make a comeback. Less is more, particularly when it comes to new plantings.

How often does one see foundation plants that are too large for the site or planted too close to the house? Why do large trees end up beneath power lines, requiring topping and one-sided amputation? This renders them not only unsightly, but prone to insects and diseases which can lead to their demise.

At our home in Alabama I planted two southern magnolia trees on either side in front in hopes they would eventually shade our house from the intense afternoon sun. Slow growers by nature, they were still on the small side when we moved away. Several years later when we returned to visit friends, it puzzled me that the magnolia on the right was twice the size of the other. But when my eye caught on the water meter by the curb and then made a beeline to the bathrooms, the mystery was solved. No doubt the larger tree had taken advantage of a slow leak at some point. I hoped my ignorance in planting a tree directly over the main water line wasn't supporting a plumber with a roto-rooter at the current owner's expense.

I've learned the hard way to carefully analyze the spot where a plant will be placed—to look up, down, and all around, to allow sufficient room for future growth. This is especially critical with trees. Even then, plants frequently have me wondering, *exactly how big do you intend to get?* Plants don't read the books to know how large they're supposed to grow and often surprise me.

The "dwarf" one-gallon Chinese loropetalum shrub I planted toward the back of my garden blew my mind when it was a tree in only three years. Although quite attractive with its vivid pink blooms and burgundy foliage, it was obviously too large for that spot. When a bad storm split and broke off major branches, I sawed the unsightly mess to the ground and bid it sayonara. To my amazement, it soon grew back into a tree.

I recently learned the term "dwarf," as used in horticulture, means "smaller than the species." In other words, if a tree normally grows 25 feet tall, a dwarf of that species might get to be only 22 feet tall. Who knew?

Like some mates, plants don't always turn out the way you wish. Once a plant is established, it's out of your control. At some point, you may have to deal with or even divorce it.

33 GARDENING WITH AADD
(ADULT ATTENTION DEFICIT DISORDER)

After breakfast I decided to water my impatiens. It was so hot and dry, they were about to croak. I washed my face, slathered on sunscreen and inserted my contact lenses. I took off my pajamas, put on some ratty jeans with Ed's old cotton dress shirt, slipped into some sandals and made my way downstairs.

In the kitchen I realized my coffee was still by the bathroom sink. I went back upstairs and took a sip—it was cold. I headed back to the kitchen and the phone rang. My sister in Pennsylvania chatted with me for over an hour. When I hung up, I remembered my coffee.

I put my cup in the microwave and made a beeline for the bathroom where I noticed the last hand towel was dirty. I went upstairs and sorted the laundry into three large piles. While putting a load of towels into the washer, I remembered my coffee. It was cold again. I pushed the beverage button and headed back to the laundry room. I loaded the washer, came back and took a big gulp—the scorching coffee scalded my mouth.

In the basement I donned my straw hat and gloves and headed outside to water my impatiens. It was getting late. The sun made me squint, so I ran back upstairs for my sunglasses. Several bills were on the counter so I grabbed them and headed for the mailbox. Yesterday's mail was still inside, including a plant catalog and a gardening magazine.

I walked down the driveway, thumbing through the magazine. Inside the garage, I stumbled over some groundcover in plastic bags that a friend gave me several days ago now in dire need of planting. I dropped the mail on the counter and headed to the basement for a shovel.

While dragging a hose to water the groundcover I planted in a holding spot in a side yard, I decided it needed some starter fertilizer, which was in the basement. I mixed up a batch and was pouring it over the groundcover when it dawned on me that I was still wearing my good sandals. I ran back up two flights of stairs for some socks before heading back to the basement to change into my gardening shoes.

After watering the new groundcover I was dragging my hose down to water my impatiens when I passed by my two goldfish ponds. The fish had not been fed in several days and were surely starving. I headed up the slope to the basement to get their food and found the can was nearly empty. I ran upstairs to the kitchen to get a new one and heard the washer buzzing that the load had finished. I transferred it to the dryer and darted back upstairs for a second bundle and put it in to wash.

Time was running out. It was good my impatiens were in back, so the yard police wouldn't fine me for watering after 10:00 a.m. I fed the fish and was about to point the nozzle toward my thirsty annuals when I saw a hummingbird take a sip from a feeder, then dart away in disgust. The sugar water hadn't been changed all week and was sour. I turned off the nozzle and took the feeder upstairs to make a refill. While it was cooling, I browsed through my latest plant catalog.

A friend called about picking up the black-eyed Susans I promised her several weeks ago. Too embarrassed to admit they weren't ready, I told her to come on and dashed to the basement. There was enough soil on hand for three one-gallon pots, so I dug them up and potted them, then doused them with some root stimulator. I was lugging them up the stairs by the deck when her SUV pulled into my driveway. As we chatted for 30 minutes, I told her it would be best to leave these plants right in their pots, keep them watered, and set them out this fall when it was cooler. *Surely they will have taken root by then.*

After she left, I was heading for the backyard to water my shriveled impatiens when a wave of nausea struck, indicating dehydration. I trudged back upstairs to the kitchen for a drink and to fill a thermal mug with ice water to take with me. The dryer bell rang, so I folded that load, switched another from the washer to the dryer, and brought the last one downstairs to wash.

Our beagle needed to go outside. I was walking Elvira on her leash when Ed came home for lunch. I made some toasted cheese sandwiches to go with tomato soup and cut some cold watermelon into bite-size pieces. The rind wouldn't fit in my compost pail, which was overflowing, so I carried it all out to the rear of Ed's garden where I buried it under a pile of dry leaves. *Will I ever find time to turn this mess over so it will make proper compost?*

As we ate our watermelon, I worked the daily crossword puzzle while Ed watched TV. After he went back to work, I folded some clothes and put the final load into the dryer. It was after 1:00 p.m., so I decided to get the mail before watering my impatiens. I waved at Terri, who was also working in her yard. She came over and we visited in the shade for over an hour.

I came back inside and remembered the clothes in the dryer. After they were folded, I made three trips upstairs to put all the laundry away. Then I took some chicken out of the basement freezer to thaw for dinner. I was putting it into cold water to thaw when the muse struck me with an idea for this book. I ran to my computer and wrote it all down before it escaped me. It was 3:30 when I finished.

I was aiming the nozzle at my desiccated impatiens when I remembered today was an old friend's birthday. I ran back upstairs to send her an e-mail greeting. Then I read the rest of my e-mails and answered two more. Before heading back outside to water my impatiens, I ate some key lime yogurt and almonds for my thinning bones.

In the distance several birds landed on my blueberries which were finally getting ripe. I decided to pick them before the critters got them. In the two hours it took me to fill half a bucket, visions of a fresh blueberry cobbler for dessert made my mouth water.

After it finished baking, I put the chicken and some potatoes in the oven and made a salad. Then I ran upstairs to get ready for my garden club meeting at 7:00.

I was setting the table when Ed came home. He looked at his vegetables, then strolled through my garden and filled his bird feeders before coming inside.

He frowned at me. "What did you do all day? I thought you were going to water your impatiens. They look like all they need now is a decent burial."

"I did, too," I said with a sigh, wishing I'd followed garden humorist Felder Rushing's advice: "The main thing is to keep the main thing the main thing."

34 COMPOST HAPPENS

Ed set the empty container down hard on the kitchen counter. "I've had it!" He snarled, glaring at me. "Don't put any more stuff in this because I'm not carrying it out there anymore. That compost pile stinks so bad I can't stand to be working in my garden. Now we've run out of leaves to cover stuff up with."

"Fine—I'll do it myself!"

The stainless steel kitchen composter was a Christmas gift to me from our daughter, who had one just like it. It resembled Oscar the Grouch's garbage can, with a charcoal filter in the lid to absorb odors. In keeping with my New Year's resolution, the past six months I'd faithfully fed Oscar every scrap: coffee grounds, tea bags, egg shells, apple cores, peels of bananas, oranges, potatoes, carrots and onions (but never bones, meat scraps, cooked leftovers or dairy). When Ed retired, I appointed him the chore of emptying Oscar in the area behind his garden where we'd piled up leaves the previous fall. Who knew Oscar would have to be dumped out almost daily? With the advent of warmer weather, corn shucks, watermelon and cantaloupe rinds required a special trip. I never dreamed the mountain of leaves we raked last fall would be depleted by July.

For several days, I carried Oscar to the compost heap myself. But Ed was right—that area was a disaster. Our practice of simply covering up kitchen scraps with dried leaves had gone from bad to worse. Felder Rushing's two rules of composting: "quit throwing that stuff away" and "pile it up somewhere" were not working for us. But it was too cold outside and I was too busy with other chores to do it right initially.

131

They taught us how to make compost properly in a Master Gardener class. The process not only involved layering, moistening and moving decaying plant matter back and forth between bins, preferably in an area with full sun, but consistent effort. I deemed this the ideal pastime for Ed in retirement, but he won't cooperate.

Various plant debris and kitchen scraps with some lime and a little water could even be placed in a heavy black plastic garbage bag for up to a year in our basement or garage. But this would be in the way, look unsightly, and could break open. Yuk!

I've about decided organic gardening is not for me. Not that I haven't tried numerous times to make black gold for my garden. However, it's in summer when I feel most guilty. Putting watermelon, cantaloupe and pineapple rinds plus corn shucks, bean and pea hulls with regular garbage destined for the city dump almost sends me to the altar begging for forgiveness.

Several years ago, after hearing yet another organic enthusiast expound on the benefits of composting vs. chemical fertilizers, I bought 60 bags of composted cow manure. Hauling and spreading it all over my garden depleted me of both time and energy. I never got around to spreading the usual 100-plus bags of pine bark mulch I typically put on my beds each spring. Though the earthworms were more plentiful the following year, so were the weeds. Whether this was due to a lack of mulch, or that the composted manure was full of weed seeds, or that we got more rain than usual that year, I'll never know. But it was reason enough for me to resume using purchased mulch and chemical fertilizer.

Although inconvenience is the primary reason I'm not an organic gardener, true organic theory claims weeds in the garden also deserve respect. They put nutrients back into the soil as well as taking them out, and are useful in insect control. Weeds are also food for numerous creatures, including humans. Interesting…but not for me. All I do to weeds is pull them. So until I become as desperate as Miss Scarlett after the Civil War, I refuse to consume or cultivate dandelions, poke sallet or any other beneficial weed. But I do feel a tad guilty.

Perennial black-eyed Susans, which steal the show in mid-summer, can get a bit weedy after several years

35 HORTICULTURAL HOLOCAUST

Disaster has struck my garden. This morning our governor declared a total outdoor watering ban for the entire state. The three-year ongoing drought coupled with rampant growth in this area has taken its toll. Lake Lanier, the chief source of water for almost four million people in metro Atlanta is at an all-time low. Lakes, streams and rivers around the Southeast are drying up. The situation is critical, meaning drastic measures must be taken. This morning on the steps of the State Capitol, our governor urged not only the religious right who helped elect him, but all of Georgia's citizens to join him in praying for rain. Ironically, this afternoon he met with yet another industry to convince them to relocate to this area and create new jobs, causing even more thirsty souls to move here.

When statewide watering restrictions were first put into place several years ago, it irked me that my odd-numbered address means I can water only between midnight and 10:00 a.m. on Tuesdays, Thursdays, and Sundays, the days I normally have morning meetings and church services. Those with even-numbered addresses may water on Mondays, Wednesdays and Saturdays. Outdoor watering is prohibited on Fridays.

It annoys me these restrictions also discriminate against the working poor. These misfortunate souls must use flashlights and risk life and limb to hand water or move sprinklers late at night or before work. Those with odd-numbered addresses might even have to miss Sunday School to water. Meanwhile, well-off citizens with automatic sprinkler systems can water sprawling lawns with ease all night and there are no restrictions on swimming pools.

But I never dreamed it would come to this. Many counties have only a 30-day supply of drinking water left. Everyone is urged to conserve in every way. All water leaks must be repaired immediately and stringent conservation measures put into place.

The governor warns cheaters will be prosecuted throughout the state. Police will be combing the streets day and night looking for illegal watering, except from wells or condensate from air conditioners. "Gray water" gleaned from dishwashers, washing machines and showers will be allowed for those on septic systems, but not sewers. All pressure washing of houses and cars at home will also cease. Only vegetable gardens can be watered legally and only at allotted times. First-time violators will be given a warning, the second time a $500 fine, and the third time, water will be shut off and a fee of $1,000 charged to reinstate service.

Rumor has it our new state motto is "Shower weekly and only with a buddy." As for laundry, clothes and underwear should be worn at least three days, sheets slept on for a month, and the family towel used over and over. A friend jokes that folks should not only put filled milk jugs or bricks in their toilet tanks to displace and save water, but all males are urged to pee off the back porch. A toilet jingle further reminds folks to conserve: "If yellow, let it mellow; if brown, flush it down."

Major religions are even reforming respective baptizing customs to comply with the new restrictions. Baptists are sprinkling. Methodists are using wet wipes. Presbyterians are giving rain checks. And Catholics are turning wine back into water.

Surrounding states are up in arms, bickering over rights to streams and rivers running through multiple states. Georgia may sue to reclaim territory that would also give them access to the Tennessee River, claiming it was mistakenly deeded to Tennessee over a century ago due to poor surveying equipment. Despite the threat almost four million humans in Atlanta could die of thirst should the situation worsen, Florida claims laws enacted by the EPA give them water rights to Lake Lanier to save their endangered mussels and sturgeons. Alabama, purportedly envious of Georgia's growth and prosperity in recent years, demands their share of the disputed water with an eye on diverting future expansion and wealth to their state. I recall tales from the 1930's Dust Bowl and fear warnings future wars will be fought over water rather than oil has prematurely come to fruition.

A tear rolls down my cheek—too bad I can't save it for some thirsty plant. I come inside and close all the blinds and curtains, unable to bear watching this horticultural holocaust happening in my haven. I try not to think of all the money wasted on plants now doomed to die and all the hours toiled in vain. Thank goodness I took pictures—I'll use them to make a scrapbook of precious memories.

I vow to join the governor in praying for rain every day. On a hunch the Native Americans also have a connection to our Divine Maker, I ravage my son's closet for the souvenir rain stick he got in New Mexico. With eyes closed, I turn the hollow stick adorned with beads and feathers back and forth. The pebbles inside it mimic the sound of rain. I hand it to my teenager and say, "Start dancing." I grab a drum and beat a savage rhythm as Bryan jumps around doing war whoops and hollers, waving the stick up and down. I laugh, mainly to keep from crying.

The drought drags on throughout the summer. The sun is scorching; the heat intense. The annuals and ferns shrivel and disappear. The grass is thin, dried and brown. Even the weeds are struggling. After my red rhododendrons succumb, I cut back my hydrangeas and other perennials so they can cope with less water, in hopes a few might survive. The trees are dropping yellowed leaves prematurely and branches are dying. I fear they'll topple when, if ever, we get another storm.

I could kick myself. Though I intended to buy several rain barrels our local Master Gardeners make to collect run-off (one inch of rain on a 1,000 sq. ft. roof provides 625 gallons), because their bright blue color clashed with my home's siding and I had neither the time nor the desire to paint them, I postponed it after we had adequate spring rainfall and the drought was thought to be over. But who am I kidding? It would take an underground cistern with a swimming pool capacity to keep a huge yarden like ours hydrated.

I am consumed with rage. Why did this state's leaders allow, even solicit and encourage rampant growth with no regard for increasing basic necessities to support it, like water? And at same time, allow the largest aquarium in the world requiring over 8,000,000 gallons of water to be built, especially with one already in Chattanooga only 120 miles away? Why is Mother Nature so destructive to her handiwork? How could the Lord let this happen after enabling me to create this beautiful space? Why? Why? Why? I stomp my foot and demand an answer.

Suddenly my deceased devout mother seemed to speak, reminding me that God works in mysterious ways and we should never question Him, for He knows best. A quote from first lady Martha Washington came to mind. After accompanying her husband on the battlefield she was instrumental in maintaining troop morale during the infamous winter at Valley Forge: "I am still determined to be cheerful and happy, in whatever situation I may be; for I have also learned from experience that the greater part of our happiness or misery depends upon our dispositions, and not upon our circumstances."

Feeling ashamed at getting so upset over the insignificance of dying plants compared to the numerous real problems of war, hunger, devastation and suffering experienced by so many around the world, I change my attitude. This total outdoor watering ban is not a tragedy. It is opportunity in disguise: a respite from dragging heavy hoses around at inconvenient times in a frenzy trying to keep things alive; a chance to replace common plants with more desirable ones whenever conditions normalize; an escape from the rigors of gardening that will give my aching body some needed rest; a gift of time to complete other chores long postponed and to pursue other interests.

Inspired with new resolve, after savoring a glassful of icy cold liquid gold from my refrigerator's dispenser, I sit down at my computer and get to work on this book.

36 BEWARE FEATHERED FRIENDS

I realized house wrens had taken up residence in a hanging basket inside our garage a second time this season when I doused my asparagus fern with liquid fertilizer. A bird sailed past my face, sending my heart into my throat. When it landed on a shrub, I could see the small brown bird, with white underside, black bars on both wings and turned-up tail was a house wren.

Tiptoeing to tilt the basket, I saw the familiar mounded nest of twigs nestled between fronds. Inside were four brown speckled eggs a half inch in diameter. Bad enough I'd doomed these future fowls to spend the night in a cold wet bed. But after Bryan informed me how critical their 13-day incubation period is, I worried they might not survive my unintentional downpour.

Upon returning from a trip a week later, it relieved me to hear chirping sounds coming from the basket. I grabbed a step stool and peered inside. Four hungry babies with yellow wide-open beaks chirped loudly in anticipation of some juicy insect morsel.

Soon the ravenous youngsters were poking their heads out, crowding the entrance, and even managing to get outside the nest.

This morning one was missing. It probably ventured out over the edge and ended up a treat for our cat. Several times in prior years a parent has fallen prey to a family pet and the eggs never hatched. You'd think from past experience they'd learn our garage isn't the safest place to raise a brood.

Perhaps different house wrens are nesting in my hanging pots each year, but I've heard they like to return to the same spot. They're known to nest in odd places, like mailboxes, garden pots, and once even the top rung of a stepladder inside our basement.

In spring, males of this migratory songbird species typically arrive a week or two before females to establish and defend their territories. They've even been guilty of destroying nests, eggs, and babies of other birds to establish their turf. After the males build a nest they sometimes stay and help females raise the brood. In fall, house wrens stop singing and retreat to woody thickets to spend the winter.

During the two-week period from the time the eggs hatch until the fledglings leave the nest, each day the babies grow louder. I rarely see the parents. No doubt they're out searching for food for their ravenous brood. Avid bird watchers claim feedings can be only a few minutes apart, even hundreds a day at one nest. Think of all the garden pests these tiny birds devour. The fact they eat such a wide variety of insects deems them every gardener's friend.

Last spring a nest of four babies hatched inside a hanging pot of geraniums overwintering in my garage. One morning I decided to take a picture of them to accompany a newspaper article in progress. It took me by surprise when I found the tiny fledglings standing at attention along the edge of the pot, as if their mother had instructed them to wait for flying lessons. By now they were used to having me check on them daily when their parents were out searching for food. They stood curiously still while I took aim with my camera at what was sure to be the photo of the year. But the instant the camera flashed, they went flying in frenzy all over. It was agonizing when I seemed to hear the babies and their mother chirping in distress the entire day.

They never came back to their nest. I felt terrible that I might have caused their premature demise, not to mention that my prized photo was blurred and ruined.

Knowing how upset I was, two days later Bryan came running in to tell me he'd spotted the young foursome by my goldfish pond searching for a drink. He reassured me the babies I'd caused to exit their nest too soon were going to be all right. I was pleased.

I hope this latest threesome inside the nest in my garage will be fine, too.

A mockingbird hovered in the redbud tree like a sentinel keeping watch. Whenever Ed or I walked up the driveway to get the morning paper or mail, the winged maniac would rush toward us screeching loudly in alarm. The first time it happened, Alfred Hitchcock's movie, *The Birds,* came to mind. *What is going on with this crazy fowl? Why is it trying to attack us?* The closer we got to the mailbox, the more frantic it would become, squawking and pecking at our clothes and hair.

Then one day I glanced down and saw a nest with three eggs inside the clematis vine growing on the trellis beside our mailbox. The puzzle was solved. The foolish mockingbird had built her nest only two feet off the ground, and was trying her best to protect it from us.

As long as the vine was blooming and the foliage was lush, the nest stayed fairly well hidden. But as clematis will, once the blooms faded, most of the foliage shriveled and turned brown, leaving the nest fully exposed to predatory enemies.

Doom, our black stub-tail cat, was no exception. The mockingbirds pounced on him in a second whenever he came by. Once the eggs hatched, they continuously harassed him, and were even more malicious toward us.

"You go get the mail. I checked it yesterday."

"No, you do it," Ed said. "Last time that mother bird parted the dozen hairs I have left. Next time she'll probably claw my eyes out."

For several days we checked the mail from the safety of our car. Then one morning I walked up the driveway without being accosted. Fearing the worst, I inched toward the mailbox. Sure enough, the nest had been violated and the babies were missing. Sadly, some creature, possibly an owl or a cat, had feasted on the fledglings, so the parents left.

We hope the mockingbirds learned their lesson and will site future nests out of harm's way. At least they haven't built one there again, and we no longer need coats of armor to check our mail.

37 ATTITUDE IS EVERYTHING

One thing's for certain when it comes to gardeners—most like to gripe and complain. Perhaps it's because gardening is difficult no matter where one gardens. Though at times they enjoy it, a garden is a huge responsibility that can turn into a burden. Almost everywhere a gardener looks, some plant is begging: "Feed me!" "Give me a drink!" "Deadhead me!" "Prune me!" "Move me!" "Do something about these bugs!"

Weather seems to be the most common lament. It's too hot or too cold; too windy or too humid; and always either too early or too late to plant. There's either been so much rain the rabbits are sprouting web feet, or so dry the lizards are carrying canteens.

If not the weather, it's the site and the soil. It's too shady or too sunny. There are way too many rocks. The soil is too sandy or it's hard-packed clay. It lacks nutrients or is too alkaline or acidic. The lot's too low or so hilly there are drainage or erosion issues.

Then there are problems with insects. Japanese beetles decimate the roses. Flea beetles feast on the green beans. Squash borers kill the zucchini. Worms riddle all the cabbages with holes. Curculio worms cause the peaches to rot. Pine beetles kill all the loblollies and they'll have to be taken out.

Next it's diseases, whether bacterial, fungal or viral. The roses and phlox have black spot and powdery mildew. Seedlings are damping off and dying. The dogwoods have blight or the apple trees are succumbing to cedar apple rust. The lawn has Army Worms, Dollar Spot or Brown Patch; it's Melting Out or just downright SAD (St. Augustine Decline).

Perhaps it's issues with varmints. Deer ravage the hostas, roses and peas. An armadillo tears up the garden searching for grubs. Squirrels devour the newly-planted tulips. Voles chew the roots off the prized peonies, causing them to topple over and die.

Frequently it's the high cost of everything. "That composted manure I got for $3.00 last year has doubled in price." "I may start growing my annuals from seed—plants that used to sell in six-packs for $1.67 are now sold for a dollar apiece, and fancier annuals are $4.00!" "It'll be a cold day in Hades when I pay $8.00 for the same perennial I got year before last for $4.00."

Gardeners who form groups complain about each other. "Why doesn't someone else take over that duty for a change?" "Old So and So doesn't know what he's talking about." "Why don't you see the light and do it my way?" "That's just not the way we've always done it around here." "Why won't somebody help me?"

Others are too critical. "She's got way too much tacky yard art." "His garden looks like a boxwood farm." "She's such a color snob—has only white blooms in her garden." "Did you ever see such a hodge-podge of plants in one place?" "Can you believe her taste?"

Some may be too selfish. Who hasn't seen gardeners who want to be the only one who has an unusual plant? According to Georgia nurseryman Mike Francis, "Gardening is a competitive sport; if I have a plant you don't have—I win!"

Gardeners also tend to get jealous. "Why did he get over two inches of rain and I didn't get a drop?" "How come she grows lavender and I can't?" "Why are his tomatoes bigger and better-tasting than mine?" "Why does she always have something blooming and I don't?"

The biggest factor affecting a gardener's attitude may be his immediate surroundings. There's always a lot happening in a garden. Something's always killing or feasting on something else. Bugs, seeds and weeds are constantly multiplying. George Sanko, a fern expert at Georgia Perimeter College Botanical Garden told us, "The garden is a place of sex and violence. Until you understand it, you haven't arrived as a gardener."

Another thing I've noticed about gardening groups is the wide variety of backgrounds when it comes to social status, religion, politics and occupations. This means gardeners may not have a whole lot else in common. Plus it is such a solitary past-time; perhaps it naturally attracts loners or those not as sociable or as tolerant as most.

Possibly because Murphy is my moniker, my garden and I seem to be governed exclusively by the old Mick's law: "In nature, nothing is ever right; therefore, if everything is going right, something is wrong!" My garden is never going to be perfect and it doesn't do me one bit of good to gripe and complain.

Yes, attitude is what's most important—in life and in gardening. From time to time I have to remind myself of Charles Swindoll's motto: "...I am convinced that life is 10% what happens to me and 90% how I react to it. And so it is with you...we are in charge of our *Attitudes*."

I'm heading out to do some positive gardening for a change.

38 WHAT WAS I THINKING?

While dragging my heavy black rubber hose down the drainage ditch to water my newest native azaleas in back, I slip and start to fall. "Dad-gum sweet gum ball," I mutter, followed by "Dear God, please help me." Somehow I avert a forward lunge and slide further down the ditch on my derriere. I'm grateful my prayer is answered. Though my wrist is throbbing and I have some scrapes and bruises, I'm all right. It's a miracle no bones are broken.

I've been feeling old and decrepit since my last check-up when I was diagnosed with Osteopenia. That's a new disease a pharmaceutical company invented after discovering a medication that would cure it. Given all the aging baby boomers, they saw dollar signs. Tests reveal my spine is more porous than my hip and ankle bones, which causes me undue concern.

Of course my bones are thinner than the women half my age in the pharmaceutical's comparison. Further tests are not needed to prove the rest of my body parts aren't working as well as theirs either. My prescription caused me such awful heartburn, after three months I quit taking it. Ironically, most medications for acid reflux cause thinning of the bones. Hello—Catch 22!

In lieu of prescription drugs, I added magnesium, increased my calcium with vitamin D, resolved to eat yogurt along with a few almonds or walnuts every day, bought some hand weights and vowed to walk our beagle three miles on non-gardening days.

I heave myself up from the ditch, wondering how much longer I'll be able to care for this all-consuming backyard colossus I began over a dozen years ago. *What in the world was I thinking? I must been out of my mind to build a garden this size with so many ups and downs.*

I blame it on the fact that something happens to a woman in that twilight zone Erma Bombeck deemed "somewhere between menopause and death." Some, like her, write best-selling books. Others, such as Grandma Moses, awaken dormant artistic talents. The most ambitious, like Hillary Clinton, aspire to the highest office in the nation but settle for Secretary of State. For me, having my last baby at age 44 with two kids already in college, likely caused a humongous hormone upheaval (perhaps to Sarah Palin, too.) Like Sarah, I took on more than I could handle. *Who knew this private sanctuary I created would prove to be a physically-demanding career just in time for retirement?*

Dragging the heavy black rubber hose with all my might I continue my trek down the treacherous gully. It hangs on a severed root. *Why in the world didn't I install some kind of irrigation system in the first place?* Struggling to untangle it, I fail to notice another sweet gum ball, but catch myself before falling. It dawns on me I'll need a stem cell transplant from a mountain goat to keep up this pace.

Extended to its limit, the hose falls 15 feet short of its goal. I turn the nozzle head to the "jet" setting and point it toward my newest native azalea. *I'm not a yard slave—I'm a jet setter!*

Turning my anger toward Ed, who is nowhere in sight, I tell him again, "That dad-gum sweet gum by the deck is a trash tree that may kill us both. See all the dead branches on it?" My eyes are on my pathetic wilted hydrangeas beneath this giant sponge that consistently steals their necessary moisture. "Those sweet gum balls are like roller skates. Someone could break his neck and sue us for everything we've got." I never miss an opportunity to warn him: "You could end up in a wheelchair;" or "How would you like to spend your final days waiting on me hand and foot for a change?"

Each time he smugly replies, "I happen to like trees." Then he reminds me we have both liability and long-term care insurance and of the small fortune it would cost to remove it. It beats me how I ever convinced this tree hugger to have two huge sweet gums in back axed after lengthy droughts caused their tops to drop out unexpectedly. It was only after I pointed out that one was blocking sun from his vegetable garden and the other was not only shading his blueberries but choking his favorite oak above the table where he sits to watch birds at his feeders that he agreed to it. What a difference it has made in both our gardens.

I flick the nozzle off and cautiously trudge up the slope, dragging the hose behind me. I turn off the faucet on the side of the house and try to be optimistic for a change. For years the prickly balls have provided harmless ammunition for backyard wars between siblings. Combined with hot glue and ribbon, they're the mother lode for Vacation Bible School crafts as well as homemade Christmas decorations for homemakers on tight budgets. New research indicates some chemical found in immature sweet gum balls may lead to a cure for dread diseases like cancer. Wouldn't it be ironic if it also cured Osteoporosis one day?

I vow to keep on keeping on, with an eye on the sweet gum balls as if they were landmines. After all, the greenest ones might make us rich one day—provided we can figure out how to get to the tops to harvest the aggravating little devils.

39 YARDEN ATTIRE

When I ripped open the envelope an engraved invitation and two tickets fell out on the countertop. As participants in our city's 2002 hidden garden tour to raise funds for city beautification projects,* Ed and I received free admission to the gala the night before the main event. The party was held in an upscale private garden that wasn't on the regular tour.

After skimming over the invitation, I looked at Ed and giggled. "It says to wear garden attire."

He grinned. "I dare you."

We'd toiled all morning trying to get everything in shape for prime time, only two weeks away. The heat was stifling, with a high predicted in the mid-nineties that afternoon. Ed's sweat-soaked gray tee shirt and jersey gym shorts clung to his body like a tree frog to a window pane. His hands and gnarly feet were encrusted with dirt. I was filthy from head to toe, with Purple People Eater hands from deadheading daylilies. We not only looked a sight, we smelled like goats!

Aside from the fact we haven't enough time and energy to take care of our respective gardens in back, there's another reason our front yard looks like a victim of benign neglect. My yarden attire looks so awful that I don't like to work where passersby might see me. That's why all the good stuff is in my hidden garden in back.

The tour and gala raised around $12,000 for city beautification, which I figure was somewhat less than the nine participants spent getting their gardens ready for it—next time it'll be a hefty donation!

It no doubt stems from my childhood. Mama's reaction to anything extraordinary regarding clothes, hairdos or behavior was, "What will people think?"

Ed claims he doesn't give a flip what other people think. "The only thing that matters to me is what *I* think," he says. Well, I not only *think* I look dreadful when gardening, I *know* I do—and it bothers me.

My mother was not a gardener and disliked being outdoors for any reason. As a teen, it embarrassed me the way she dressed when hanging clothes out to dry, as if the sun might cause radioactive burns. The small lots in our subdivision in New Mexico meant the houses were close together and someone was nearly always out in their yard. She'd put on one of Daddy's old long-sleeved plaid shirts over her print housedress and a homemade calico "Sunbonnet Sue" with a brim larger than mule blinders. Mama explained to me once that although she and her girlfriends worked in the fields of their Texas family farms of necessity during the Great Depression and 1930's Dust Bowl, having tanned skin was proof they had, and something respectable young ladies of that era would never admit, even to each other.

These days when I'm out working in my garden, I look ten times worse than Mama ever did whenever she hung out clothes. Ed's huge old long-sleeved cotton dress shirt with tattered jeans, clodhopper shoes and holey socks is more my style. A wide-brimmed straw hat, sunglasses and colored gloves that don't always match complete my ensemble. Due to pesky bugs and intense sun, I keep myself covered up from head to toe. In my younger days my skin would tan but now it gets spotty. I'm allergic to pesticides and fragrances in most sunscreens. By covering up with cotton clothing, these can all be avoided.

Another reason I don't like to be seen when gardening is because I get so filthy. One might even mistake me for the grandmother of Charlie Brown's friend, Pig-Pen. I doubt there's a soul around who gets as grungy as I do. It embarrasses me to be seen like that.

I've always envied my friends Diane and Marilyn who care for plots near mine in our Buffalo Creek Demonstration Garden. On a Master Gardener workday, Diane will come dressed in a pink shirt and shorts with matching visor and white socks and sneakers. When it's time to leave, she looks almost as good as she did when she arrived. It's the same with Marilyn. How they manage to stay so clean is beyond me.

Like it or not, there remains a double standard. A female landscaper once told me about stopping after work to get milk for her kids. The cashier gave her filthy, disheveled self the once-over and said, "My, aren't we dressed up today." No doubt she wouldn't have uttered a word to a male landscaper.

There's a stigma it's not lady-like to be outside doing anything more strenuous than planting petunias or cutting roses. Digging with picks and shovels is men's work. Whenever a former pre-school neighbor would see me working in my yard, she'd come over and tell me, "Miss Shelly, you should hire someone to do all this yard work for you."

It's hard to be a proper damsel in distress when you're 5' 12," taller than your would-be male rescuer whom you may outweigh as well. Given my height and strength, it's futile to try and appear weak and pitiful like my short mother, who longed for a life devoid of drudgery. I feel silly waiting for some feeble older man two-thirds my size to open a door for me in the name of chivalry, although I do cooperate to appease them.

I've not only been blessed with good strength for a woman, but lots of willpower and determination (aka hard-headedness). It enables me to lift and situate rocks, dig goldfish ponds with a pick in Georgia's packed clay, hack at stubborn limbs and roots, and heave 40 pound bags of composted manure as a bona fide AARP qualifier. I like to see tangible results for my efforts—a spotless house or a meticulous garden, not merely a toned body acquired indoors on boring equipment for a fee. It will be a cold or rainy day indeed that finds me exercising at a gym while others watch me sweat. Besides, the money I save can be spent guilt-free on new plants.

Two years ago my daughter asked me to come out to Washington and help her design a garden between her new deck and master bedroom addition. When Laurie added, "and bring your garden clothes," I reminded her garden designers wear silk and linen. We slaved all week putting in a goldfish pond, digging out grass, building beds, setting stepping stones and shopping for plants. Laurie planted everything after the exterior was painted. When we visited there the following summer, her new garden was in full bloom and looked beautiful.

Asking for a show of hands when speaking to a garden club makes it easy to target my audience. If most of the ladies have designer fingernails, they're primarily tea-sipping flower arrangers. If they're serious nitty-gritty gardeners, their hands and nails will look like mine and those of most other Master Gardeners.

I once gave a novice gardener a start of almost every perennial that could be dug up and divided. She planned to come and help me dig them, but since she had another appointment that morning, I got an early start before it got too hot. Over 75 plants were dug and ready to go when she arrived just before noon. It amused me that she came to help me dig wearing nice clothes and good thong sandals with a fresh pedicure, a gold ankle bracelet and even a toe ring!

The afternoon of the aforementioned gala, following a quick shower, I soaked in our Jacuzzi tub for nearly an hour to get the grunge out of my nails and pores and to help rejuvenate my tired aching body. And in consideration of other guests, Ed and I did not wear our usual yarden attire.

40 X-RATED PLANTS

I slammed the newspaper down in disgust. It was preposterous that a judge in Michigan, a state with 10,000 natural lakes, was allowed to decide the fate of almost four million people by ruling that in three years Atlanta would no longer be allowed to use Lake Lanier for its drinking water.* Never mind there are no viable alternatives since Georgia has no natural lakes. With the current recession causing drastic budget cuts in every category, the ruling came at the worst possible time.

Though my own Carroll County had the foresight to build reservoirs to meets its needs, I had visions of it being forced to sell its water to Douglas County and on down the line until it reached Metro Atlanta. This would no doubt result in statewide total outdoor watering bans.

I tried to imagine an all-native garden filled with drought-tolerant perennials like hearts-a-bustin' and bare naked ladies, but no thirsty preachers in the pulpit;** a lawn of Astroturf sprinkled with islands of cacti and colored gravel; and beds and pots filled with fake flowers. The mere thought made me shudder.

According to NBC Meteorologist Paul Ossman in Atlanta, "Weather is a study of extremes that always averages out." Lake Lanier's situation is proof he's right. During the last three-year drought, the lake got so low that some predicted it would never be full again. By

---

*Two years later in 2011, this ruling was overturned by a judge with better sense.

**Use caution when searching for these native plants on the internet—you could be accosted by cardiologists, pornographers and religious fanatics!

2008, things got so critical statewide total outdoor watering bans were instigated. I bid every astilbe, fern, azalea and hydrangea in my yard adieu. In order to help perennials and larger shrubs cope, I cut them back and removed all moisture-competing annuals. After mulching everything well, I crossed my fingers.

To my surprise, next spring most every perennial in my yard reappeared, including those moisture lovers presumed dead. Even the ferns were resilient. I suspect it was because my plants were so well-established. My practice of infrequent but thorough watering gave them extra deep roots.

One year later in 2009, thanks to adequate precipitation followed by torrential September rains in the Atlanta area (which lamentably caused ten deaths and damaged 20,000 homes and businesses), once again Lake Lanier filled to the brim. The drought was thought to be over.

It's now the first week of fall, 2010 and things have never looked drier. Rainfall has been sporadic in the hottest summer I can remember here (more than 90 days of temperatures over 90 degrees, even into fall). There hasn't been a decent rain now in over a month and there's no relief in sight. Trees are sporting dead branches and dropping leaves so fast few will be left for fall color. Though total outdoor watering bans are not in place yet, I'm worried.

Can anything be done to have a beautiful yard in spite of drought? Although good design, proper soil preparation and frugal watering are necessary for success, plant selection is crucial.

Several years ago when I complained of drought, a friend in Colorado told me about an X-rated plant program out West. Since my yard is on a slope and I'm somewhat lazy when it comes to watering, it didn't surprise me that many plants on that list were already growing in my yard (although I'm mindful that some may do poorly or even die in prolonged wet periods). The "X" refers to "Xeriscaping" or designing with water conservation in mind. Depending on drought tolerance and the amount of water required to thrive, plants are tagged at garden centers as X-rated (1" per week); XX-rated (1/2" per week); and XXX-rated (1/2" or less every two weeks).

These days it's easy to find out almost everything I ever wanted to know about a plant but didn't know who to ask. A list of drought-tolerant plants for my area is available from my state's cooperative extension service office and its website.

I plan to get X-rated now and put some more eXcitement in my yard!

41 GARDEN THUGS

For years each spring I've planted impatiens around my ponds and waterfalls in partial shade. When they get leggy in early July, I fertilize and cut them back. Soon they have lush new growth that looks good until frost. Lately, I'm having second thoughts. In shady areas impatiens are prolific re-seeders, especially on paths and between stones defining my terraced beds. Without frequent watering, they look pathetic. I failed to trim mine this past July and by fall many were two feet tall and crowding out perennials. Next year I may substitute low-maintenance begonias or vinca around my waterfalls and send these thirsty thugs on furlough.

Within two years the cleome (spider flower) seeds a friend gave me were coming up all over my sunny terraced beds and choking my perennials. Last spring when seedlings covered bare spots like a carpet, I pulled up five bucketfuls. All summer I yanked out every one I saw so none would go to seed. But this year they were back, making me sorry I ever planted them.

I also regret taking the first violet from a well-meaning friend who adores and cultivates these petite invaders. Though not unattractive, they reseed with abandon in my lawn, on my paths and between stones. I'll be grappling these incorrigibles forever.

Most pond plants get intrusive. After learning how invasive chameleon and Gooseneck loosestrife can get, I finally eradicated them with consistent effort. One or two water hyacinth and water lettuce have multiplied and covered the surface of my ponds several times in a single season. Floating plants like anacharis, which help aerate the water, also get too thick. In sharp contrast, I can't keep parrot's feather since my goldfish devour it.

Mint should be confined to pots or better yet, in the yard of a least-favorite neighbor several houses away. If conditions are right it spreads like molten lava.

Ornamental grasses have also been a problem. Pampas grass was originally planted on either side of our front yard near the street. Through the years, the shade of maturing trees sent one into steep decline but the one in full sun is huge and continues to spread. It requires cutting back in late winter, an annual chore I've come to dread. No doubt it will take nuclear weapons to get rid of it. Though unsightly, a heavy black plastic tarp secured by big rocks might kill it eventually.

Research indicated some "yard grass" a friend gave me was Miscanthus sinensis, and I planted it in three spots around my ponds. Though quite attractive, within three years it grew too large. Hard rains splayed it all over the ground and the task of tying it up was daunting. The clumps were beasts to dig out but I finally moved one to a shady spot in back which keeps it manageable. My experience with zebra grass from a plant swap was similar. I've replaced these grass thugs with variegated cascading sedge about a foot tall that never has to be cut back.

Groundcovers are some of the biggest culprits. The usual scenario is the first year it sleeps; the second year it creeps; and the third year it leaps. When we moved here I brought along two pots of geraniums with three sprigs of English ivy. I rue the day I planted the ivy under our deck. Within three years, it not only covered the ground and was headed up our deck supports and brick foundation, but that area was also a mice habitat. After learning English ivy can ruin mortar on brick walls and even kill trees, I ripped it out. Over the years English ivy has crept up from the woods and taken over our wild area in back. Last year we hacked it from native trees. This winter the plan is to banish it forever, but its thick, glossy surface renders weed killers ineffective and it will require manual digging.

To save on annual mulching, pachysandra seemed ideal to use around azaleas and hostas. I realized too late this attractive groundcover was not a good choice. Though it competed well with tree roots, it choked my hostas and azaleas. It took some effort to dig it out and after three years sprouts still appear.

The variegated vinca major I planted in the island of trees between our yard and a neighbor's to discourage weeds is now generally regarded as invasive. The vinca minor I planted on the opposite side is much better.

I've never grown bamboo, but some hefty stands grow in yards around here. There are many varieties, both clumps and running types. The latter are rampant spreaders and said to be the fastest growing woody-stemmed plant in the world. Hopefully, Atlanta's zoo will want it to feed hungry pandas.

Deep in the woods in back Chinese wisteria is rampant. Each spring it's a sight to behold with its stunning foot-long lavender blooms. But its long thick vines twine around and smother trees. I have visions one day of suckers running clear up the hill and invading our subdivision. Instead of the destructive Asian varieties, I planted the native 'Amethyst Falls,' American wisteria, which has smaller blooms on thinner stems, although pruning is required to control its size and shape.

Though our slope has no low, moist spots, I still keep an eye out for kudzu. This Japanese vine imported in the late 1800's to control erosion can grow up to a foot a day, with roots 12 feet deep weighing up to 300 lbs! This thug swallows up trees and even parked cars and houses. It does have some merit for making bio-fuels, baskets, and for feeding voracious goats.

I wish now I'd sought some vine advice before planting a trumpet vine to cover a large unsightly stump a decade ago. By the time it grew to any size the stump disintegrated. I moved the vine to the back where it scurried 50 feet up the trunk of a tulip poplar and bloomed several years later. But suckers continually spring up from the original site as far as 40 feet away. I've dug them out and sprayed them with weed killer, but the more I do the more there are. I'll be at war with this enemy longer than the U.S. is with the Middle East.

Years ago I got an obedient plant at a plant swap. Eleanor saw this ironic misnomer and warned me it would consume my entire lot. Though disappointed, I got rid of it. A while back I was pleased to find a new hybrid obedient plant bred to behave itself and bought two one-gallon pots at $8.00 apiece. The one planted in full sun bloomed a lovely pink by mid-summer but in its second season covered an area six foot square. The one in shade didn't grow much and finally bloomed the second season, but the following spring it also began to spread. Was this a misfit that failed to hybridize and reverted back to its origins? Or was this obedient plant sold as a hybrid when it wasn't? In either case, I'm tempted to take a trunk full back and demand a refund.

I've learned the hard way (how else?) to be careful when selecting plants and the spot to plant them, and also to be wary of plants from well-meaning friends. If they've done well enough to share, sometimes they turn out to be invasive.

42 DOOR PRIZE SURPRISES

We drooled with anticipation as the man on the stage pulled a slip of paper from a basket. "A Solar Genome goes to...Shelly Murphy!" Though I was thrilled my name was among the first drawn for a door prize at our fall Georgia Master Gardener conference, the long trek to the front had me wondering...*exactly what have I won?*

To my dismay, the man merely handed me a coupon with instructions to claim my prize in another room when the meeting ended. Though I faked a smile, I knew the day-long suspense would be excruciating.

During lunch I mentioned hearing that DNA tests could now be done on plants. Results were useful in determining if a patented hybrid had been pirated by unscrupulous propagators and sold as another cultivar.

"I never heard of such a thing," a woman across the table from me said.

"It's true," I said, turning to my friend Carol. "You think my prize is some new solar-powered gizmo that scans and identifies genes in plant DNA like the government's Human Genome Project?" She shrugged.

"If so, do you think they'll want me to collect DNA samples on every plant I have and report the results?" Carol shrugged again. "It's too bad they didn't have it in time for euphorbia 'Diamond Frost.' I heard that plant was pirated and sold under a different name."

"It's probably happened with lots of others, too," Carol said.

When the meeting ended, I rushed out to claim my prize. I was slightly envious as those ahead of me walked away with the latest hydrangeas, camellias and other beauties. After muttering a polite thank-you, I took the lightweight cardboard box to the bench where my friends were waiting. Like me, they couldn't wait to see a Solar Genome.

The moment I pulled out my prize, we all cracked up. It was a squatty plastic elf with long nose and red pointed hat holding a silver gazing ball that collected power from the sun all day and lit up at night. Indeed, I'd won a Solar *Gnome* for my garden!

I had recently assumed the stance "less is more" and sometimes too much when it comes to yard art. Three adorable leprechauns Laurie gave me already resided in my garden. On the way to the car I announced the prize was up for grabs—and thankfully it was.

I read the label on a foot-tall green plant I'd just won as a door prize at our fall Master Gardener conference. "It's an *Amorphophallus konjac*—I've never heard of it have y'all?" My friends shook their heads. I couldn't wait to get home and look it up, and hoped it was hardy in my Zone 7b.

After having no luck finding it in several gardening books, I searched the internet and learned *Amorphophallus konjac* or Glucomannan, is commonly called devil's tongue, elephant-foot yam, voodoo lily and snake palm. In Asian cuisine both the corm and tuber are prepared like potatoes or noodles, and also used as a sweetener. Though the human body cannot digest *A. konjac*, because it is low in calories, high in fiber, and contains many vitamins and nutrients, it is helpful in treating diabetes, high cholesterol and obesity, though it has warnings and must be used with supervision. It is also used as a food preservative and a thickening agent for pharmaceutical products and cosmetics.

Despite the fact the flower can produce an offensive odor like rotting flesh or a dead goat and the tuber can get up to 50 pounds, my curiosity was tweaked. For some reason, I thought the plant was tropical. But before I could transfer it to a larger pot and move it inside, the foliage withered and died. I banished the pot of dirt to the basement, not overly disappointed since it was free. Plants that aren't hardy aren't popular with me since I lack a good spot to overwinter them.

It seems there's never enough dirt around when plants need repotting. Although experts recommend using new potting soil every time, that's too much trouble and expense. I figure dirt is dirt. So if it is fairly good soil, I save it in my basement and reuse it. So far, there hasn't been a problem. Such was the case with the pot of soil that housed the deceased A. *konjac*.

The following spring when I dumped out the contents, to my surprise a monster tuber resembling a patty pan squash tumbled out. A row of 1½ inch white roots around its scalloped edge meant there was still hope. It had simply gone dormant for the winter. Since it was past the last freeze date in our area, I planted it by our deck which seemed the perfect spot to observe it.

Several weeks later a thick reddish shoot appeared, only to be broken off the next week by some unknown culprit. Though I was disappointed and expected it to die, I kept watering it just in case. In late June another shoot came up and by September the plant was two feet tall and wide, but still no sign of a bloom.

Oddly enough, near the new arbor we installed the previous June where soil on hand had been used, two more A. *konjacs* came up. I was puzzled. A website informed me that A. *konjacs* are hardy in zones 6-10; the bloom appears first thing in spring before the leaves; and they don't have to bloom to produce offspring!

In early November the plants froze. The next May when they still had not reappeared, I figured our unusually cold winter had killed them. However, in mid-June, every one of the shoots broke through the ground. And on the other side of my yard, another A. *konjac* sprouted. *What is going on with this voodoo weirdo?*

Since A. *konjac* did not appeal to me as cuisine, my better judgment told me to discard every tuber in my yard, including the mother. But given my curiosity to see and smell the bloom, I left the original tuber intact. I did rip out the offspring for fear they might overtake my entire backyard.

One day this past spring, we noticed our beagle sniffing and circling that spot. Sure enough, the attraction was an exotic foot-long dark red sprout with putrid odor. From the four-legged nose's reaction, it did smell like a dead animal and Elvira's curiosity kept her going back to it for a week. Since one had to get close to it to fully appreciate the smell, I showed the bloom to several friends. It grossed them out. Within a couple of weeks it shriveled up and disappeared.

By July, however, there was a clump of familiar green foliage four feet tall and wide comprised of eight or nine shoots. Whoa! This plant was behaving like Octomom! Though an interesting conversation piece, it was way too risky to keep any longer. I dug it out, put it in plastic bags and threw it in the trash. Frankly, I'd enjoyed about all of it I could stand.

The man on stage at the conference announced the lucky Master Gardener would receive some worm castings, and pulled out my name. By the time I got to the front, another winner had claimed my prize by mistake. The helpers apologized and gave me a coupon to pick up my ligustrum 'Howard' after the meeting since it was currently being used as a stage decoration.

I thought of our home in Alabama with nine ligustrums across the front that got so large we hardly needed window coverings. It took constant pruning to keep them from obscuring our home's entire front facade. Since my current yard was running out of space, I hoped Howard was a dwarf cultivar bred to behave and couldn't wait to get home and look him up.

My heart sank when I saw Howard. He was over three feet tall and wide in a huge pot. Though robustly healthy with lush glossy foliage, I wondered how I'd lug him out to the car. When my friend Lynn saw me wrestling him off the stage, she volunteered her husband to help me. Thankfully, Dennis came to my rescue.

When ligustrum was not listed in my plant encyclopedias' indexes, I was puzzled. In the section on broad-leaved evergreen shrubs in my *Better Homes and Gardens Complete Guide to Gardening,* when I found ligustrum listed under "privet," however, I was shocked. Surely they didn't give me an invasive reseeding pest that folks are urged to annihilate.

No, ligustrum 'Howard' must be a good cultivar, even if he hails from the privet family. One must not judge a person or a plant by his relatives. The donor is a reputable and generous southern nursery. Except for being evergreen, Howard hardly resembles his thuggish wild cousins in my woods. I gladly sacrificed a damnina at the edge of my yard and planted Howard there. The book claims he'll make a good screen...so I'm keeping my fingers crossed.

43 A DECENT BURIAL

There's a trick I learned from our oldest son who is a medical doctor. Like doctors, gardeners can bury their mistakes! That's right. If a plant succumbs or is ailing or simply doesn't do well for me, I just yank it out of the ground, dig a hole, and hide the evidence.

Through the years I've saved tags from almost every plant I purchased. Now I have a bucket full, enough to fill a book of precious memories. That's exactly how many are now classified.

I recently went through this bucket of labels. It was astounding how many have kicked the bucket. Before sending a plant to its final resting place, I like to give it a postmortem inspection, akin to a human autopsy. I always proceed with caution, however, since that plant that looks half-dead could still be half-alive.

One of the most common causes plants die is that they were planted in the wrong spot. My earliest victims were 25 bare-root tea roses that came in the mail with metal engraved dog tags as clues they might eventually succumb in combat with enemy forces. Though not impossible to grow in Georgia, my yard was a poor spot. Tea roses were too high-maintenance for me. They not only required gigantic amended planting holes, but constant watering, fertilizing, spraying, deadheading and pruning. Their treacherous thorns snagged my arms and clothing. Deer, Japanese beetles and aphids loved them, as did unsightly black spot and mildew. The smelly chemicals required to treat their ailments were offensive to me and the environment. When persistent drought with a total outdoor watering ban in their fifth year caused them to decline to the point of utter despair, I performed a mercy killing. Though the Knockout roses I replaced them with also get too large, have treacherous thorns, and are favored by deer and Japanese beetles, they are otherwise low-maintenance.

Replica of Savannah's famous Bird Girl
surrounded by Knockout Roses

Like patients deprived of oxygen will gasp for air, plants can suffocate when too much soil and mulch is piled around their necks. I planted my first hybrid azaleas too deep, which smothered them to death the first season. I accidentally piled too much mulch around my spiderwort and succulents and the crowns rotted.

Many of my plants died because I failed to first analyze their needs. My flowering quince never blooms because it was planted in too much shade, although deer eat what few buds it has in late winter. Several daylilies and irises have steeply declined due to encroaching shade from maturing trees. I have lost Joe Pye Weed, corkscrew willow and cardinal flower due to insufficient sunlight and water. Since I garden on a slope, nothing has died from root rot due to soggy soil or standing water although it has killed several of my houseplants.

Diseases have caused the demise of others. Sometimes it's hard to determine the problem since symptoms are so similar. Fungal and bacterial diseases can be treated, while viral diseases cannot. I normally discard leaves affected by powdery mildew in the trash. My bee balm and phlox are favorite targets of this malady. After enjoying vinca annuals for years, mine promptly died due to a virus. For several years vinca could not be found for sale as growers developed disease-resistant varieties. My state's cooperative extension service and its website have information on treating specific diseases. Directions must be strictly followed, just like a doctor's prescription.

I learned early on that my packed red Georgia clay will need amending. Adding aged pine bark or composted manure makes the soil friable which enables the roots of annuals and perennials to breathe. At the same time it helps preserve moisture and allows for good drainage. However, experts now recommend that shrubs and trees be planted in native soil that has been thoroughly loosened or tilled in a wide area so the roots will spread out and better support them to maturity.

Just as a patient can be overfed or improperly medicated, plants can suffer and even die from incorrect fertilizer or a soil pH that is too alkaline or acidic. In recent years, I've planted a dozen native azaleas. Sadly, only one has done well and three of the five planted recently have already expired. After learning mushroom compost (my lone soil amendment on hand at planting time) has an unusually high salt content, I wondered if it rendered the soil's pH unsuitable for them. Or they could have gotten too little or too much sun or water. Who knows? I suspect native azaleas are as tricky to establish as they are to propagate.

Climate is a huge factor. Just because a plant is sold in my area does not mean it will do well here. I admit to killing two dwarf Alberta Spruce and I am not alone. One supplier of these upright conifers to a chain of home improvement stores estimates folks in Metro Atlanta alone kill about 8,000 every year. Years ago I planted two of these petite evergreens in large concrete pots on my front porch in full sun. This is why mine did not survive their first summer and the reason I did not replace them. The key word here is Alberta, as in Canada, which has cooler temperatures they require. On the other hand, I've grown Russian sages for years. While visiting New York one summer, at first I did not recognize the full mounded shrubs with lush periwinkle blooms as being the same plant. Now it's obvious that life in Georgia's intense heat has been a struggle and my Russian sages will never reach their full potential here. In sharp contrast, my Siberian irises are as persistent as weeds despite neglect. Just further proof some plants are more heat-tolerant than others.

Wooly thyme and lavender soon give up the ghost for me. Although both herbs are supposedly hardy in zone 7, they dislike our warm, humid nights. They also prefer well-drained sandy soil, the exact opposite of our native packed red clay. I also love delphinium and Irish moss, but know they will incinerate due to heat and humidity. Whenever I see a stranger with any of these in their cart, I'm tempted to say, "Don't waste your money." Sometimes I do give free advice while shopping. So far no one's told me to mind my own business. I also use such opportunities to learn from others.

I adore annual lobelia and once planted a dozen in a clay strawberry jar on my deck. It was a whole two weeks before they melted and vanished. Last spring I bought a new heat-tolerant variety for a trial. With frequent watering, it did all right in a large pot on my deck. But when June temperatures soared into the nineties, it promptly bit the dust. I may try this petite-flowered indigo beauty again in a spot with no afternoon sun in hopes future summers won't be so scorching hot.

After admiring a friend's perennial 'Heat-Wave' hyssop, late in the season I planted two pots I found on sale in full sun. Come spring mine were stone dead, but hers survived. The fact mine were not well-established likely caused them to succumb to the coldest winter I can remember here. Or perhaps hers had more protection. Every yard has micro-climates; the lower the area, the colder it will be. My slope may be cooler in winter than a flat yard on higher ground.

Established but tender perennials (meaning they prefer zones 8 and higher to my zone 7b) such as shrimp plant, ice plant and 'New Gold' and purple lantana also froze to death last winter. I feared my angel trumpets, purple heart and purple oxalis were also history but they were just late reappearing due to an unusually cool May.

Though it's hard to admit, I'm also guilty of malpractice. I failed to remove a wire plant tag around a rhododendron's main stem which cut off all its nutrients like a tourniquet and it died of starvation. Several times I've lost my balance and my clodhopper feet accidentally trampled seedlings to death while my derriere squashed a few others. Because I lacked pruning expertise, shrubs I butchered were made more susceptible to insects and disease. I went on vacation in mid-summer once and several new plants died of thirst. More than once, I've yanked out a weed only to realize it was a pricey new perennial.

Extreme caution must be used with chemicals since sprays can drift and kill desirable plants. A Japanese maple in our Master Gardener demonstration garden likely succumbed due to prolonged drought and/or through uptake of weed killer sprayed beneath it and on nearby paths. Years ago, we used a lawn chemical company until they accidently annihilated a small pink dogwood and some newly-planted annuals.

Just as diagnosing a patient's problem can befuddle the best doctors sometimes it's hard to pinpoint what ails a plant. After five years my native bottlebrush buckeye has grown only slightly and never bloomed. Though it's at the edge of trees and gets morning sun, it constantly struggles. I've watered, fertilized, and even scored around its roots with a shovel, as a native plant enthusiast suggested. Perhaps it's atop a giant buried rock or tree roots are choking it. Maybe it's simply inherited midget genes. For whatever reason it's stunted, this winter I plan to move it in hopes it will thrive elsewhere. If it dies, so be it. It's better to lose it than to endure continuous frustration.

Like human beings, some perennials simply have shorter life spans. I've heard a perennial is a plant that, if it doesn't die the first year, may come back the next. Those with short life spans for me include white coneflower, coreopsis, and hens & chicks. It's comforting to know their early demise was due to genetics and wasn't my fault.

I've even had problems with plants designated as Georgia Gold Medal Winners, which are supposed to thrive here with routine care once established. Purple 'Wave' petunias consistently wave goodbye to me; six one-gallon pots of creeping raspberry croaked the first season; and purple 'Homestead' verbena that likes to roam has left the premises.

Though finding the right plant for the right spot will always be a challenge, it's fun to experiment. Besides, mistakes are easy to bury.

At least I thought interment was a cinch, until our largest Leyland Cypress turned a sickly shade of green before it shriveled and died. Evidence the virus is spreading upsets me. Soon the most prominent feature in back will be an unsightly row of decaying giants. They were clearly a poor choice for that site. Years ago we were clueless that such small trees would get so large. Prolonged droughts and the fact we planted them too close together and never fertilized reduced their vigor and made them prone to disease for which there is no cure. They're too large to bury and will be expensive to remove. I wonder...would cremation be an option?

44 FAT CHANCE OF RAIN

I've grown weary of weather forecasts. Media predictions of a 10% or 30% or 50% chance of rain are so frustrating. Rarely do they say there's a 100% chance, at least not that I can remember, we've been in drought mode for so long. Sometimes I get the urge to snatch that perky weather gal with big boobs right out of the TV, shake her by the shoulders and demand, "Tell me bimbo, is it going to rain at my house today or not?"

A week ago last Tuesday when a 60% chance was in the forecast, I decided to be optimistic for a change. Though highs hovered in the nineties all week, I was so busy I passed on my appointed watering day under Georgia's current restrictions, hoping Mother Nature would give her handiwork a dousing. Though we got thunderstorms that evening, not one drop of rain fell.

It didn't rain on Wednesday, either, even though there was a 40% chance. Ed and I drooled with envy as we watched the Atlanta Braves head for the dugout some 50 miles away as tarps were rolled out onto the field for a one-hour rain delay on television.

On Thursday, the prospects were 50-50. With two meetings that day and another that night, I crossed my fingers and passed up my appointed time again. All we got were ominous clouds and rumbling thunder.

Even with a 40% chance on Friday, it stayed dry as Mama's cornbread, and hot enough to pick fried green tomatoes right off the vines.

By Saturday, predictions were exactly the same. My plants were so pathetic I was tempted to call 911. My huge native trees were dropping leaves like prolific dandruff; my hydrangeas drooped worse than a teenager's baggy jeans; and my impatiens looked scalded.

I decided to cheat. What difference could it possibly make which day I watered when neither of my contiguous neighbors ever watered their yards at all? I sneaked up my long crooked driveway and looked all around to make sure no one was watching. Switching the two with the three on my mailbox sign turned my odd-numbered address even. Now it was legal for me to water that day. That morning I hand watered in back for four hours, and did another five hours after supper, using a flashlight to finish up. Then I switched my address back so we could be found in case of emergency.

Only a slim chance was predicted on Sunday, but the following week looked promising. I got up early and watered for three hours which made me late for church.

Now that everything was watered except for our parched Bermuda lawn, I was certain we'd be deluged with rain on Monday or Tuesday. Though clouds gathered both days, temperatures hovered in the mid-nineties and not one drop of precipitation fell.

On Wednesday, with a 40% chance of rain in the forecast the next three days, I noticed deer had nibbled my roses, phlox and hostas. I mixed up a gallon of expensive liquid deer repellant, knowing full well it would wash off in a rain. Spraying all my deer delights using a quart spray bottle took two hours and blistered my fingers. I figured reapplying it was a small price to pay for a good rain. Again, nothing happened.

By Friday my plants were as melted as lobelia in Louisiana in August. I told Ed to get the car washed. "And don't put it back in the garage. Leave it out on the driveway. That always works." This time it didn't.

Our entire yarden was at the critical stage by Saturday. In lieu of cheating to water it all again, I decided to wash all the windows. In the seven years since we'd gotten replacements that can be washed on both sides from inside the house, this would be only the third time I'd done it. Afterwards, for extra measure, I took a king- and two queen-size comforters to a laundromat with huge front-loading washers. I brought them home and hung them on my deck rail to dry. Surely now it would happen. Though heavy clouds loomed overhead with several claps of thunder, once again the fickle finger of fate failed to point our way.

By Sunday, my garden needed life support. I not only prayed for rain before, during and after church, I invited a friend who's an impeccable housekeeper to a cookout that evening, even though I'd spent the week writing and my house was a mess.

"Aren't you afraid it will rain?" She asked.

"I hope so, because I plan to dance in it." I stopped by the store after church and spent the afternoon preparing food and clearing a path downstairs. Despite a 60% chance, the event happened without a hitch.

Early next day, my plants seemed to cry out to me in agony, "Either give us a drink or call the likes of Dr. Kevorkian—just put us out of our misery." I tore myself away, took refuge inside my air-conditioned house and closed the blinds.

Next morning over coffee I told Ed, "We should give up gardening. All this heat, drought, bugs, deer and weeds—why do we torture ourselves like this? It takes me 15 hours just to water my ornamentals, dragging hoses from plant to plant. We simply cannot keep this stuff alive without rain."

He shook his head. "My zucchini got stewed and my corn's about to pop. I'm afraid to dig up my potatoes for fear they're already baked. My peppers and okra are tough as rawhide. No matter how much I water, it's not the same as rain. Only a 10% chance today."

I batted my hand at him. "Phooey on chances! I may water my perennials but my annuals are history. I'm not hosting anything else at this sprawling inferno."

Late that afternoon when it got cloudy and windy, I didn't even get my hopes up. Thunder and lightning didn't excite me, either—until 6:35 when large drops began pounding the deck. I closed my eyes, put my hands together, turned my head toward the heavens and begged, "Pl-e-a-se dear Lord...let it pour for 20 minutes." Lightning cracked and thunder boomed, though the sky wasn't very dark. By 7:00 the gutters were overflowing and water was racing down the ditch in back. At 7:25 it stopped, but it drizzled throughout the night. Next morning when our rain gauge indicated almost three inches, I uttered a prayer of gratitude.

I've had it with weather reports. I'm hanging a weather forecasting stone on a rope right outside my screened porch like the one I saw on the main street of a quaint little town in Vermont. First thing every morning, I'll poke my head out the door. If the stone's dry—it's a clear sunny day. If wet—rain. If dusty—a sandstorm. Hard to see—fog. White on top—snow. Jiggling up and down—earthquake. If the stone's plumb gone—a tornado!

45 IF NOT NOW, WHEN?

"I will *not* be a hoarder; I will *not* be a hoard—"

"You're talking to yourself again, Shelly," Ed said.

"It helps me get rid of this junk. That show about hoarding on *Sixty Minutes* was a real eye-opener."

We moved so often the first 25 years we were married I disposed of junk on a regular basis. But here, it was easier to banish old stuff to the basement than to haul it off. Cleaning out this space could not be postponed another minute.

The path from the stairs to the back door was narrowing by the day due to overwhelming clutter. It was hazardous for all who dared to enter and also dark because there was too much junk beneath the lights to get a ladder in to change the burned-out fluorescent bulbs. Several times we had stumbled, but didn't fall. I hoped with Ed's help, it would take us three days.

"First, let's break down and recycle every cardboard box," Ed said.

I frowned. "Have you any idea how hard it is to find boxes for mailing gifts to the kids and grandkids?" I pointed to a stack of boxes six feet wide, tall and deep in the back corner. "Don't throw those out until after I look at them. These days, for computers and electronics, you have to return defective stuff in their original boxes."

Ed picked up a giant square box. "No way am I keeping this monster."

"That's for my leather office chair—if it breaks it must be returned to the store in that box or else the warranty won't be good."

"Well, I've sat my big behind in it plenty of times and it's still intact," he said, tossing the Styrofoam packing aside. He collapsed the box and heaved it at the pile. "Just let me handle it—they'll take it back. What about those big boxes over there?"

"Those china barrels cost a small fortune each time we moved. No telling what they are now."

"Well, I won't fit in 'em, and whenever I move from here, it will be in a box!"

"I never throw those out. They're the best for storing stuff. Go organize your fishing gear."

He looked at me in disgust. "Take your time, there's no hurry. This stuff's only been piling up down here for 17 years." He wiped his brow and grumbled, "How does a family of three collect this much crud?"

He slashed a large box and an avalanche of Styrofoam pellets flooded the filthy floor.

"Now look what you've done! Picking this up will be a career move," I scolded.

He glared at me. "What in the hell are you saving this stuff for?"

"You think I save it on purpose? I've tried throwing it out. It fills up the hobo, leaving no room for garbage, plus it blows all over the yard when it's hoisted over the truck. There's another giant boxful in the corner. Sometimes I use it to take up space in the bottom of large garden pots so they'll need less soil. I'll use some in August when I ship Kristen's birthday crystal. Why don't you recycle it? Some shipping stores will take it if it's clean."

"I refuse. Tie it up in garbage bags—it's going to the dump. I'm going to check the Braves' score. Let me know when you get this stuff picked up." He trudged upstairs and turned on the TV. Soon he was snoring.

Later that afternoon he took two pick-up loads of cardboard to be recycled and another load filled with assorted Styrofoam to the dump.

Early next morning he moved two bicycles and larger gardening items outside—hoses, lawn edging, two garden carts, a wheelbarrow, a lawn mower, a tiller, a spreader, a weed eater, and seven large empty buckets. While Ed ran some errands, I cleared the carpenter bench of all gardening debris, seeds, plant tags and tools. Then I sorted all the screws and nails.

Later we moved the tool bench and pegboard to a different wall. I began the ominous task of organizing all the carpenter tools and hardware, which took two more days. Again I suggested he tackle his fishing gear.

I carried a box of magazines outside and pulled out several issues of *Southern Living*, some dating back to 1993. No wonder I kept them. The covers had beautiful gardens, homes and food—three of my favorite things. I tried to thumb through one but the musty pages were stuck together, no doubt due to the 20 inches of rain we got in four days the year before. Our basement hadn't been the same since and still smelled musty, no doubt because of yucky stuff like this. I put them in a pile and got nine more boxfuls—*Home and Garden, Better Homes and Gardens,* and *Traditional Homes.*

Worthless painting supplies were next, including a bucket of leftover wall spackling, nine cans of dried paint, seven used rollers, spent sandpaper, three tubes of dried caulking and a half-dozen petrified brushes.

Ed eyed the wall of shelves filled with his camping and fishing gear. "Why is it so darn dark in here?" When he saw the basement windows were covered with black landscape fabric, he rolled his eyes at me and said, "No wonder."

"I nailed this up the last minute before my garden club came last week. I'd die if anyone saw this mess." I ripped it down. "I always figured this stuff was good for something. It sure didn't block any weeds. They either came up through it or grew on dirt that piled on top. Guaranteed for 20 years—what a joke!"

Three boxfuls of various metals destined for recycling were next—old copper ice-maker tubing; worn-out faucets, door knobs, plumbing and light fixture parts (some stainless steel and solid brass); rusty lawnmower and weed eater blades; a bent wrought-iron chair; and a hatchet with a missing handle. *Too bad I can't get this stuff to that artist who welds junk like this into amazing yard art.*

I eyed two broken shelves—the plastic one held Bryan's childhood toys. The metal one with wood graining was the first thing we acquired as newlyweds for our humble abode. It took six months to save enough green stamps for it. *So many memories.* Ancient fungicides, pesticides and herbicides filled the shelves. As beginning gardeners, we'd deemed them necessities, even for Ed's vegetables. We hadn't used such items in years. I tossed them out along with five cheap garden sprayers that broke the first or second time they were used. Were it not for the fact every chemical must have its own sprayer, I would have invested in a good one.

Old Christmas decorations were next. Two porch trees made from tomato cages and fake garlands, complete with lights were sacrificed as were gold and natural pine cones, dried hydrangea blooms and crumbling baby's breath. I flung several rolls of soiled ribbon, crushed velvet bows, and plastic fruit from my *della robbia* decorating craze onto the pile. Two boxfuls of mildewed door mats, straw wreaths and ornaments, raffia ribbon, and paper Maché deer and angels followed. When I told Ed a box of ornaments with peeling paint were from our very first Christmas together and he pretended to play a fiddle, I tossed them out too.

I stacked up five china barrels full of porcelain Christmas villages and accessories against the back wall. *Why did I ever get myself into this expensive, bulky, and useless collecting phase? It's Aunt Shirley's fault, for sending Bryan a North Pole collection. After that we were hooked. Maybe I can sell them on E-bay some day.*

Ed saw me standing on tiptoes trying to hang a gigantic Christmas wreath I'd made from an old hula hoop, fake garlands and a string of lights. I usually embellished it with fresh greenery from our yard.

"What are you keeping that for? We always go see the kids at Christmas now."

"What if we didn't?"

"Don't tell me we can't celebrate Christmas here without this fandangle." I sighed and handed it over.

Ed pointed to a blue plastic kiddy pool. "That's history—our grandkids are too big for it now."

"No! I put my goldfish in it while I'm cleaning my ponds."

"This sucker would hold a whale!" He wrestled it out the door. "Put your darn fish in a plastic bucket."

Ed hauled off an old armchair, a wooden rocker and an antique bench beyond repair. I moved another wooden rocker and a rattan swivel chair to a corner for us to sit in during tornado warnings.

Despite Ed's protests, I refused to part with some wooden shutters, a lattice screen and our old oak front door and two sidelights with oval leaded glass. Seeing architectural relics while touring a garden designer's home and business, convinced me these treasures would look great in my garden some day.

Two tattered wooden screen doors, pieces of odd lumber, a decrepit lampshade, a busted hamster cage, a broken vacuum, a Styrofoam cooler, a torn green hamper, and a cracked laundry basket filled up another truckload. Ed had it all tied down when I had second thoughts. "I'd like to keep one old screen door for sifting soil to remove rocks."

"Over my dead body," he said, and drove away.

Ed came back and pointed to a shelf. "Let's toss out those old birdhouses."

"No, they're practically new. One is a bat house kit you got for Father's Day and haven't put together. The big plastic high-rise we never put up is for Purple Martins. Both would help remedy the mosquito problem around here. I got that blue bird house when I spoke to a garden club. It needs to be at the edge of a field."

"No doubt you've noticed we don't have the edge of a field. Are you waiting for a tornado to make us one?" I stuck my tongue out at him.

Ed perused my gardening stuff and shook his head, "When are you going through this mess?"

"Right after you finish organizing your fishing gear that's covering half the basement over there. That's where I plan to put all my garden stuff."

I began removing junk from the old tool monster he'd built from plastic lattice and two-by-fours. Like most do-it-yourself projects, it sounded better than it worked. "Look, Ed—here are my missing red pruners!"

"It's just like Christmas morning down here," he said with sarcasm.

A pick-up full of stuff was set aside to donate to my Master Gardener group, including a planting cart for our demo garden and dozens of black pots, 16 glass vases and 37 woven baskets that would come in handy for future plant sales. I also sorted and set aside stacks of black pots and holders for plants I planned to donate.

I put several blue and green wine bottles into a box for recycling. *Given my allergies to nitrates, I'll be room temperature before I save enough for a bottle tree.*

While Ed went to buy more tool hangers, I used a dolly to move several partial bags of concrete, sand and assorted ceramic tiles and grout. *Someday I'll make hypertufa pots and decorative concrete leaves, and put mosaic on my benches and stepping stones.*

When Ed came back I couldn't wait to tell him the good news. "Guess what? I also found my black ergonomic pruners! They've been missing for ages."

"It's like a darn archeological dig down here," he quipped.

After searching 30 minutes for the drill, we installed the new tool hangers. Ed brought the gardening tools inside and I hung the best ones. It was great. Now we could find whatever we wanted. I threw out several cheesy broken tools, including an $80.00 tree limb pruner that bent the first time it was used. I learned the hard way (is there any other way?) it doesn't pay to buy cheap tools. Sometimes even pricey ones are duds.

Ed picked up some pieces of yellow foam and frowned. "This looks like part of a mattress pad."

"That's exactly what it is. No one sells replacement filters to fit my big flower pot pond filter anymore so I cut large circles from that pad and an air conditioner filter. They work just as well, plus it saves you a ton of money."

He faked a grin. "That makes me so-o happy."

After mating up a pile of gloves I discarded those with holes along with several tattered straw hats and 35 mud-encrusted stiff old shoes.

It took 15 trips to the dump and the better part of 10 days to purge, straighten and clean our basement. Though there was still plenty of stuff we might never need or use again, at least now it was semi-organized chaos.

Before Ed hauled the last load to the dump, he came back inside to see if I could possibly part with anything else. He picked up two red and blue foam noodles Bryan used for swimming as a teen. I'd forgotten to ask Bryan if he wanted to keep them. I couldn't resist. "Hold on to those. If you join them end to end with an oil pan in the center, you'll have floating planters for your pond."

"You can also twist 'em around your wife's neck and choke her to death," Ed said, heaving them like spears right by my head.

46 IT'S UNTHINKABLE

The worst has happened—my beloved husband suffered a fatal heart attack while planting his winter garden, so it came as a shock to all. Married when I was 19 and he was 22, I can barely remember when Ed wasn't a part of my life. Despite differing backgrounds that had friends and relatives predicting a marriage between two so young could never last, love and perseverance held us together. We raised three successful children and stuck it out through thick and thin over four decades to prove them wrong.

Our kids, grandkids, my siblings, several cousins and all their families came here to be with me. Sad how spread out we are, never able to get together until tragedy strikes. If any good can be gleaned from losing a loved one, it is the camaraderie of family and friends.

Months after the fact, I'm still grieving. At Ed's memorial service, it consoled me to hear his many career accomplishments and the difference he made in the lives of youngsters he mentored. They honored him by establishing a memorial scholarship for future athletes at the last university where he coached basketball and served as athletic director for 16 years. I still run into people around town, even strangers, who stop and tell me nice things about him or how he touched their lives in some way. Several have told me how much they miss the fresh tomatoes and other vegetables he shared with them every summer.

The thank-you notes have all been written. Friends were wonderful, offering support in so many ways: staying with me until relatives arrived; shuttling kinfolk back and forth to the airport; helping me plan the memorial service; making memorial donations; sending cards and flowers; and bringing in food—who knew cream of chicken soup and cool whip were so versatile? The last of the funeral food relegated to the basement freezer after everyone left is still there. My appetite has vanished.

His estate has been settled, a relatively simple task due to his careful planning. Thanks to him, I should be all right financially, barring some worldwide economic catastrophe. Since I always ran the household, paid the bills and did the taxes, I don't feel as discombobulated as most widows. Although I still cannot bear to watch *Jeopardy* alone. Because we never shared the same interests or went many places together even after he retired other than to a ball game or a restaurant, not much has changed with my routine. But I'm still as sad and lonely as that "One Love Bird" must be that was for sale in yesterday's paper.

In accordance with his wishes, I clutch the urn tightly and carry it down the stairs across the lawn to his garden. A coach to the core, his affinity for the sport assures me he'd approve of the basketball urn I selected.

Despite the fact it's a cold windy day in March, I see him standing between his raised beds aiming a hose at his green beans. He's wearing his tattered straw hat and one of a closetful of tacky gray tee shirts I always detested with baggy polyester gym shorts and flip-flops. I call his name and walk towards him, intent on reminding him to water more deeply. After all, I'm the Master Gardener in this family—why won't that stubborn man ever listen to me? I blink and he disappears.

The last of the three beagles Ed owned after moving to Georgia almost trips me. His hounds were constantly "gettin' loose," much to the chagrin of a persnickety neighbor or two. Truth be known, he couldn't stand seeing his pets penned up like derelicts. He delighted in their shrill incessant barking as with new-found freedom they chased varmints from our property into the woods. I reach down to pet Elvira, his favorite, who no longer requires a leash. Since her master's death, she rarely leaves my side. She misses him as much as I do.

As I lift the latch on the massive wooden gate, a streak of brilliance flashes before my eyes. My wedding rings are still on my left hand. The last thing I need is to be accosted by some old geezer looking for a nurse with a purse who can cook and clean. The top hinge on the bulky gate is broken, just like my heart. I manage to heave it open and we go inside.

It dismays me to see Ed's garden overflowing with dead debris. What in the world will I do with 30 raised beds surrounded by an unsightly eight-foot deer fence with green metal poles and ugly gate? After concentrating on ornamentals for so many years, I have neither the desire, stamina, nor need for such a large vegetable plot. A few herbs and a couple of tomatoes in pots on the deck will suffice for me.

I'm feeling old, old, old...nearly dead. Surely it will take hired help this year to get my own flowerbeds cleaned up, fertilized and mulched. Professional landscapers are too expensive and today's teens are too lazy for manual labor. I've always been opposed to hiring illegal immigrants. Besides, I likely couldn't communicate what needs to be done. Next week, for my own good, I should put this place up for sale and downsize to assisted living. Lord only knows how many days I have left above ground.

It occurs to me our home's original oak door with oval leaded glass is in a dark web-infested corner of our basement. Although we replaced it after it could not be repaired, I could not bear to part with it. Why not hire a handyman to tear down Ed's fence and raised beds and recycle the oval door and side panels into an attractive structure along the back? Adding lattice and sturdy posts with fancy finials will transform it into an outstanding backdrop in white for a new formal garden. Small boxwoods can be planted in a geometric design in four quadrants separated by gravel paths bordered in bricks. A massive concrete urn on a pedestal overflowing with seasonal annuals will grace the circular center. What a fine parterre it will make! By bringing the structure forward several feet, the old chain-link dog pen can be hidden behind it, as well as a compost bin in full sun in a final attempt at going totally organic. I might even host small weddings in the garden or turn this place into a bed-and-breakfast! I can't wait to start designing it.

My eye catches glimpse of the urn and guilt consumes me. My aging body collapses into an old rusty green chair around the table of the first patio set we ever bought. It was Ed's favorite resting spot while working in his garden. I set the urn on the table and burst out crying. There's a hole in my soul that will surely never heal. Sensing my pain, Elvira licks my arm and starts whining. I pet her as we cry like hired mourners at an Italian funeral.

Minutes later, I wipe my tears away and carefully remove the lid. I hold it in my hand for a moment...then put it back on. I thought it was time, but it's not. I'm not ready to let him go.

I hear snoring and reach across and touch his chest—it's warm! My heart leaps as cold chills go down my spine. Ed's alive! Thank God, he's alive! After staring into space for several moments, I snuggle next to him, put my arm across his chest and close my eyes. Tears of joy stream down my cheeks. My Rock of Gibraltar stirs, but does not waken. Still shaken, I heave a sigh. All is well.

But I'm hanging on to that oval door…just in case.

Shelly H. Murphy

RESOURCES:

Better Homes and Gardens Complete Guide to Gardening

The Georgia Master Gardener Handbook, Fifth Edition,
Cooperative Extension Service/The University of Georgia College of
Agricultural and Environmental Sciences/Athens

The 400 Best Garden Plants, a practical encyclopedia of annuals, perennials, bulbs, trees, and shrubs by Elvin McDonald

The Southern Living Garden Book. The Complete Encyclopedia of more than 5,000 Southern Plants

Amorphophallus Konjak: www.ehow.com/about_4672320_what-amorphophallus-konjac.html

Tansy: http://en.wikipedia.org/wiki/Tansy

Martha Washington's quote on happiness:
http://www.famousquotesandauthors.com/authors/martha washington_quotes.html

Anonymous quote on life: http://www.dictionary-quotes.com/

Murphy's Law quote on nature: amirite.net/473677

Charles Swindoll's quote on Attitude: www.bigeye.com/attitude.htm

Verbal quotes from speakers Mike Francis, Felder Rushing and
George Sanko were from the author's notes taken at Master Gardener
meetings